Kitchen Table Lingo

Kitchen Table Lingo

A first book of home-made words

Written and edited by Bill Lucas and
Edward Fennell
with Richard Brooks

Foreword by Melvyn Bragg
Afterword by David Crystal

Published by Virgin Books 2008

2 4 6 8 10 9 7 5 3 1

First published in Great Britain in 2008 by
Virgin Books
Random House, 20 Vauxhall Bridge Road,
London SW1V 2SA

www.virginbooks.com
www.rbooks.co.uk

Addresses for companies within The Random House Group Limited can be found at:
www.randomhouse.co.uk/offices.htm

The Random House Group Limited Reg. No. 954009

A CIP catalogue record for this book is available from the British Library

ISBN 9780753518199

The Random House Group Limited supports The Forest Stewardship Council [FSC], the
leading international forest certification organisation. All our titles that are printed on
Greenpeace approved FSC certified paper carry the FSC logo.
Our paper procurement policy can be found at
www.rbooks.co.uk/environment

Printed and bound in Great Britain by
CPI Bookmarque, Croydon CR0 4TD

Acknowledgements

This book is the result of many people's passion and enthusiasm for the English language; thanks everyone, you are all **avlexly**!

The Committee of Hyde 900 & Julian Chisholm who began it all.

All of our distinguished celebrity contributors.

KTL word-checker-in-chief Alys Blakeway with Madelaine Smith and Sam Byford.

Ben Francis and TheMediaSet who provided invaluable software.

The University of Winchester, especially Mary Fagan, Professor Joy Carter, Tommy Geddes, Corinne MacKenzie and Trish Kernan.

Winchester City Council, especially George Becket, Simon Eden, Sue King, Eloise Appleby and Marilyn Michalowicz.

Hampshire County Council, Hampshire Library Service, Ken Thornber, Yinnon Ezra, John Clarke, Matthew Haynes and his team, Russell Cleaver and Bob Wallbridge.

Michelle Davis and the Heritage Lottery Fund.

Lord (David) Hunt, Simon Hodson, Robin Fry, Michael McManus at Beachcrofts and Michael Lynd at Marks & Clerk.

Our wonderful PR company Spada, in particular Gavin Ingham-Brooke, Claire Wordley and Tali Robinson.

Mark Byford, Pat Loughrey and Mia Costello at the BBC.

Our English Language gurus – Professor David Crystal, Sir Christopher Ball, Professor Bas Aarts, Professor Clive Upton, Kate Brett, Valerie Mitchell and Susie Dent.

Richard Dixon and Ben MacIntyre of *The Times* and Richard Brooks of *The Sunday Times*.

The English Project trustees, steering group and Hampshire friends – Professor Christopher Mulvey, Dominic Hiscock, Evelyn Thurlby, Edward Fennell, Professor Bill Lucas, Paul Hodgkinson, Sarah Murray, Barbara Yorke, Paul Williams, Lucy Wolverson, Baroness (Celia) Thomas, James and Alice McConnachie, and Josie Dixon.

The *Hampshire Chronicle* and especially Warwick Payne.

Annabel Merullo, Tom Williams, Alexandra Henderson and all at PFD.

Louisa Joyner and Davina Russell at Virgin Books.

But, most important of all, the thousands of English-speakers from all over the world who have contributed their Kitchen Table Lingo.

Foreword

MELVYN BRAGG

Broadcaster, novelist and author of *The Adventure of English*

The English language is unusual in that it follows a double-track, having both the literature and language in harness from the early eighth century. *The Lindisfarne Gospels* were written then by the monks in Latin – the official language. A subversive Anglo-Saxon translation was added in ink above the Latin.

So we had an English vernacular language written down well before other European countries. We also had in the eighth century the influence of somebody as important as the Venerable Bede, urging his followers to write Anglo-Saxon.

I speak of a double-track, but in a way it has sometimes been triple. There was the official language written in books; the written vernacular; and the spoken – the language which came from the fields and the streets of the day, and still does: this can be called the Kitchen Table Lingo of today.

We have also benefited from writers like Chaucer, who was key. He knew English, Latin and French. But he chose to write in English. This was a major turning point. So English, after the Norman Conquest, entered imaginative literature.

The greatest chronicler and inventor of words that were then written down was Shakespeare. He used words from fifty different languages and even invented – in that we had never seen them written before – more than 2,000 new words. What we have to remember is that Britain at that time was becoming a major trading nation not just in goods but also in words.

Historically, our language has been singled out by other nations as a truly great language. Take the Brothers Grimm, two Germans who in the early nineteenth century argued that English was special because it combined Romantic, Germanic and Scandinavian. This factor, I think, will be central to The English Project in Winchester.

What is happening now around the world is the development of E2 – the second language of the globe. This is abbreviated English, which is used in particular in the worlds of business, sport and diplomacy. It is a blunt version of English. And then there is the constantly developing English local language with its different dialects from Wessex to the West Indies. Hinglish has developed – a mix of Hindi words and phrases with English – or Singlish, a dialect from Singapore that mixes English with the native Chinese and Malay.

As a spoken language, English is unpretentious unlike, in particular, French, which is very controlled. The French language changes slowly and, though the French might use a few English words like 'le weekend', their aim seems to be to keep the barriers high between print and the spoken word.

Another aspect of English is that we like language which teases. Our humour is often based on innuendo and double entendre. Yet it still matters that we have the Oxford English Dictionary. We need the established, official language. But it is equally important that the OED is not the only lingo.

The great thing about our language is that it is dynamic. It is almost uncontrollable. In fact, it is speeding up now faster and faster through text and email language. And while I still know that for many the apostrophe matters, it is words and the sense they provide that are most vital. English changes all the time – some words last for a short span, some for much, much longer. Some stick. Some flop. But the language is always alive.

Guest Contributors

Robert Adam

Anne Atkins

Simon Armitage

Melvyn Bragg

Jilly Cooper

Leo Cooper

David Crystal

Hunter Davies

Susie Dent

Mo Farrell

Margaret Foster

Kathy Lette

Sir Trevor McDonald

Ian McMillan

Rosie Millard

Deborah Moggach

Philip Pullman

Meera Syal

Alan Titchmarsh

Jeremy Vine

Introducing The English Project

Bringing together this first collection of Kitchen Table Lingo may be a small step in the history of the English language, but it's a **bedooftey** leap for The English Project!

Our aim, as a registered charity, is to help English-speakers across the globe become more aware of where the language has come from and how it continues to develop. Underlying that mission is a strong belief that English belongs to the people who speak it. It's not the dictionary-makers or academics who own the language, but the people like you who are on the front line day-in, day-out using and extending it.

English is a great, inclusive inheritance that all of us can enjoy. And Kitchen Table Lingo is a way of acknowledging publicly the fundamental contribution made by individuals who shape the language in their homes and workplaces to express new ideas and change the language so it works better (and more amusingly) for them.

But there is much more to come.

Looking ahead, The English Project has many other ideas which it is cooking up. Based in Winchester, where King Alfred the Great took momentous steps in establishing English more than eleven hundred years ago, we will be creating the world's first visitor attraction devoted to exploring the unfolding stories of one of the world's great languages – English. If you visit our website at www.englishproject.org, you will start to get a fuller picture.

Meanwhile, enjoy your Kitchen Table Lingo.

The Trustees
The English Project
www.englishproject.org

Can your words pass the Kitchen Table Lingo test?

Every day millions of English-speakers use words that are not to be found in the dictionary or the newspapers. They are words passed down through friends and families or which have been recently invented to meet a new need. Or sometimes they have been coined just for fun. Most often they are found in the home. That's why we call this informal vocabulary Kitchen Table Lingo or KTL.

The English Project has been collecting KTL, and this book contains a selection of the words we have enjoyed most.

In order to qualify as KTL the rules are simple:

✓ the word must *not* appear in authoritative dictionaries (or at least not with the standard dictionary meaning)
✓ it must have been in use amongst three or more people (in other words it's not just lovers' gooey talk)
✓ it must have been in use for at least a month (so it's not just a flash in the pan)
✓ it must NOT have been invented simply to get into this book (because that would be cheating)
✓ it mustn't be a brand name (because that's just a rip-off)

Every word that is submitted to Kitchen Table Lingo is individually checked, although we cannot (sadly!) visit you in your home in person. We are relying on you to be straight with us. But we do look very hard at the dictionary. If your word does not meet the KTL test then we will tell you why.

Ultimately, though, Kitchen Table Lingo is about enjoying and celebrating the rich potential of the language and the creativity of English-speakers. If all this sounds a bit serious, don't worry. Throughout the book we have left spaces for you to jot down your own KTL words, so you can be the ultimate judge of whether you have satisfied the rules! Just go to www.englishproject.org/ktl and add your word. And who knows, one day your word might end up in a 'proper' dictionary!

A

Accifault *noun* something that was your fault that you would rather was an accident

'Why do **accifaults** always happen to me?'

Andrew Stone sent us this, and his family has been using it for the last three years, although he claims that it is really the invention of his kids.

Aganaut *noun* an upper-middle-class housewife, usually from the Home Counties, who owns an Aga and spends her life walking dogs, playing tennis and gossiping with other aganauts

'AGANAUT: I just love my Aga!

ENVIRONMENTALIST: But don't you worry about the fact that it's on all the time?

AGANAUT: Don't be silly dahling; it's really very green.'

The Crane family.

Aggranoyous *adjective* what you'd call someone who was being really difficult

'Can't you just stop being so **aggranoyous**!'

Howard Richards.

···

Anagipta *adjective* feeling sick, usually due to alcohol

> 'I feel so **anagipta**. I don't think I'm going to make it in to work today.'

Simon Robson and some fifty of his friends use this word, mostly in Yorkshire and London, although he doesn't tell us what they say when they are caught between north and south.

···

Arker *verb* to listen

> 'Just stop talking and **arker** to me!'

Sarah Newton and her 'mam' use this to ensure that they arker to each other. Dorothy Scaglion and her family have been using it since 1935 on the Isle of Wight.

···

Asqueviate *verb* to adjust to a situation

> 'Yet again Charles showed his unique ability to **asqueviate** to the new arrangements.'

David Whitmarsh.

···

Attentionise *verb* to pay undue attention to a person or an animal so as to cause a change in their behaviour

> 'Lucky's impossible whenever you **attentionise** her. She completely forgets she's a dog and starts behaving like a spoilt child.'

Madeleine Cuff and her family in Brighton.

Avlexly *adjective* so lovely that other words fail to describe the loveliness

> 'You beautiful, wonderful, gorgeous, sexy person you. You're so **avlexly**.'

Peter Smith and his group of friends use this when their powers of imagination fail them: 'The pinnacle of loveliness. If something is avlexly, then it cannot be more lovely or more perfect.'

Add your own KTL word here

word _____

definition _____

sample _____

_____

B

Babob *noun* an annoying person, especially an upholder of petty or obstructive bureaucracy

> 'You may say I'm a **babob** but I say I'm just doing my job.'

Francis Bown, whose family and friends use it when confronted by irritating bureaucracy.

Barmbedarm *noun* a large filling breakfast or the bloated stomach that follows

> 'I'm feeling so full – I've just had a great **barmbedarm**.'

Liam Buckley: 'One day in a greasy café we were eating a large fried breakfast and "Black Betty" was playing on the radio, and we sung along to it, changing the words to Whoa, big belly, barmbedarm and it just stuck! From then on, every time we ate a large breakfast or felt like we had a large protruding belly, we called it a barmbedarm.'

Bazungle *noun* face

> 'This is the last time I want to see your **bazungle** around here.'

Rob Eady, who made it up; it is now used in his household.

Beans *adjective* an alternative to 'cool'

> 'Those new jeans are so **beans**.'

Lucy Taylor and her friends used this at college and it has continued since then.

Bear-farm *noun* a bad joke that leaves an awkward atmosphere

> 'Not so much a shaggy dog story, more a **bear-farm**, isn't it.'

Toby Hiscock, who uses it with friends following an incident in which a long conversation about bear-farms was continually interrupted by bad jokes.

Bedooftey *adjective* something which is so big – usually referring to a bodily part – that words like huge or massive cannot do justice to it

> 'Seen the bloke with the **bedooftey** bum?'

Chemaine Walters tells us that 'When my husband started work as a butcher at Safeway in Ilkeston, this word was a slip of the tongue but it just stuck. He used it in each new store he went into and it was picked up by others, including me. That was twenty years ago, and it is still in use'.

Bejoist *verb* to spring suddenly from out of nowhere

> 'Kate didn't have a chance. The paparazzi just **bejoisted** on her, cameras flashing.'

E. Caloe thinks it just sounds like the perfect word to describe the action and uses it with his friends.

Belm *noun* a lie

> 'Yorkshire beat Lancashire! That's a **belm**.'

Ronnie Irwin, who says that it is used by secondary school children in East Lancashire. 'The word is often said whilst forcing the tongue in to the lower lip to extend the chin. "Belm" is exclaimed when one suspects a lie has been stated. One who lies may be outed as a belmer.' Rest assured there are no belms in this book.

Berwyn *verb* to claim knowledge of a subject or topic despite overwhelming evidence that the speaker or writer really knows nothing about it

> 'Of course, Gordon Brown used to **berwyn** a lot about how to be a successful prime minister.'

Brian Perman, who explains that 'Berwyn was the name of a cottage that a member of the Perman-Turnbill family had never seen but nonetheless described in great detail with great inaccuracy'.

B'ganky *noun* a large handkerchief

> 'She's got a cold – give her a **b'ganky**.'

Malka Baker, as used by the Sanders, Holloway and Baker fam?ilies with their children.

Bibbly *adjective* pleasantly drunk

> 'Couple of glasses and I'm already **bibbly**.'

The Russell family.

Biggoron *noun* a long process, usually with multiple steps, designed to achieve a single outcome

'OK, it's going to be a **biggoron**.'

Matt Rea says this is popular amongst the gaming community.

Bill's mother's *noun* threatening weather conditions

'Just as we broke open the champagne it started to look dark over **Bill's mother's**.'

Pauline Heywood, who isn't certain about the origin but whose family has always referred to the appearance of approaching bad weather along the lines of 'It's looking black over the back of Bill's mother's.'

Billy *noun* a travel guidebook

'Look it up in the **billy**.'

Derived by Ian Doody and his friends Sue, Rose and Steve while travelling around Turkey. Inspired by the idea of 'Billy No Mates', i.e. someone with no friends.

The story behind **bic-a-bonnet**

Bic-a-bonnet *noun* sodium bicarbonate

Kit Merrill and his sister grew up using the word **bic-a-bonnet** for bicarbonate because they learnt it at their mother Marjorie's knee. She in turn almost certainly learnt it from her 'Granny Ida', a semi-relation with her roots in the Victorian era but who looked after the young Marjorie as a child in Scarborough. 'I imagine it was due originally to a mishearing or misunderstanding by someone who perhaps couldn't read,' explains Kit. But it illustrates how family traditions – the simple handing on of words from one generation to the next – can take us back rapidly into the world of the nineteenth century.

North-East Connections
Like a lot of Yorkshire folk, Kit Merrill has a deep interest in language, especially that of his native county where so many varieties and dialects and sub-dialects lurk. He remembers, for example, going out when young, into the Esk valley near Whitby and coming across a local lad whose native tongue sounded more like Norwegian than English, testimony to the rich history of the language.

Indeed, Kit emphasises the connections between the north-east and Scandinavia. He recalls a long boat trip across the North Sea to Sweden in the 1950s. His travelling companions turned out to be a Geordie, whose accent Kit found almost impossible to understand, and a Norwegian woman. This was in the days long before Scandinavians spoke English as a matter of course. However, the Geordie and the Norwegian woman had enough words in common to make themselves understood fairly easily. 'I was stuck in the middle like a gooseberry being able to understand neither of them,' says Kit. In return, they probably could not have understood **bic-a-bonnet**.

Bimbensioner *noun* a superannuated bimbo, 'mutton dressed as lamb'

> 'Do you fancy her? I think she's a bit of a **bimbensioner**.'

Rick Hulse.

Bimble *verb* to travel or go idly without purpose, agenda or restraint of time

> 'What do we do as Members of the European Parliament? Well, I suppose we **bimble** around mostly.'

John Tode, who recalls that, while he was a boss of a team of six people working on a countrywide project, the word suddenly cropped up during a business meeting. 'It was used by a Yorkshire lad, who, when I queried it, said that the whole team was saying the word, it having crept quietly into their conversations over a period of many months. I now use it all the time, the word seemingly self-explanatory when used.'

Bimmer *noun* TV remote control

> 'Pass me the **bimmer**!'

Louise Dermont. First coined by her late father but used by 'my mother, sister and I and anyone who lives with us'.

Bindorria *noun* a refuse truck, or any other council vehicle

> 'I was stuck behind a **bindorria** for half an hour.'

Matthew Abercrombie.

Bingle 1. *noun* the alternative event, activity or party you organise when rain forestalls your original plan:

> 'We were going to have a barbecue but it rained so we had a **bingle** instead.'

2. *verb* to bingle, meaning to continue a party indoors

> 'The weather was atrocious but we **bingled** instead.'

Al Firrell. 'Because it happens a lot we thought a word was needed,' says the Firrell family.

Bippon *abbreviation* 'I beg your pardon'

> '**Bippon**! I didn't recognise you for a moment'

Kate Williamson, who explains that it was used by her husband's grandmother, who was from West Yorkshire and was born in about 1910.

Birkenhead *expletive* just the kind of thing to say when something goes wrong

> 'Oh **Birkenhead**!'

Marcus Ainley. Used for over forty years by the extended Ainley family.

Bisk *noun* a jolly or holiday as used by brokers in the City of London

> 'I'm off for a **bisk**.'

John Ronan.

What do you call it?

Can you believe it? In the very early days of broadcasting you actually had to get up from the sofa and switch the television on or off. But for the last fifty years there's been no reason to be anything other than a couch potato and reach for the **bimmer** (or any of the other words in this book)!

The earliest recorded example of a remote control was invented by Nikola Tesla in 1893. A US patent describes a 'Method of an Apparatus for Controlling Mechanism of Moving Vehicle or Vehicles'. Snappy title, huh?

Back in the 1940s lazy car drivers wanted a way of opening their garage doors without them having to get out of the front seat, and the idea of the remote control as we know it was born.

Then at the Zenith Corporation in the 1950s various early prototypes were developed, first the 'Lazy Bones', then the 'Flashomatic' and finally the 'Space Command'.

Fast forward to today. Maybe it's because there is something deeply unsatisfactory about the words 'remote control' or perhaps it's because television is such a central part of people's lives; for whatever reason, KTL words for the remote control have been rolling in.

Clicker and Zapper have been around for a while, but what do you think about the selection here? Which is your favourite? Why do you think 'remote control' is such a weak name? **Tell us at www.englishproject.org/KTL**

We've included dozens of words for remote control in this book but could have added dozens more – here are just some of the examples we've seen!

'Pass me the…'

Bimmer, Blapper, Blitter, Blooper-dooper, **Boggler**, **Bomper**, **Bumper**, Buttonbox, *Butts*, **Cajunka**, Channel changer, Channel-panel, **Clicky**, Commander, Conch, *Dibber*, Dibbler, **Digotrondit**, Dobar, Doflicka, **Donker**, Doobery, **Doofer**, Dooty, *Flicker*, Flipperdopper, **Flugel**, Funnyding-dong, **Gum gum**, *Hoofer-doofer*, **Kadumpher**, **Mando**, Melly, *Mutilator*, Norm, Oofahdoofa, Phaser, *Pilot*, Pinger, Plinker, **Plinky**, Pokery, Podger, Potiater, Presser, Pringer, Rees-Mogg, Remy, *Splonker*, **Spurgler**, Squirter, *Telly box*, **Tinky-toot**, Turner-upper, Twanger, **Twidger** , Wanger, **Widger**, Wiz-wiz, *Woojit*

Bissou *adjective* gross, disgusting

> 'That is so **bissou**!'

Emily Colton and family.

Bist *interrogative* the question 'Are you?'

> '**Bist** going to the pub?'

Nick Gibbons. Used as local slang in the Dawley and Wrockwardine Wood areas of Telford. Bist enjoying Kitchen Table Lingo?

Bizzle *noun* a short period of time

> 'I'll start my homework in a **bizzle**.'

Nazreen Akhter: 'It was created in a conversation at school. We were having a laugh and I just came out with it. It has stuck ever since!'

Blangy *adjective* feeling off-colour for no specific reason with no real symptoms

> 'Don't want to go to school. I'm **blangy**.'

Anne Knight, whose family and friends use it. They attribute it, maybe libellously, to the 'French town name thought to be an appropriate description of the feeling.' Fortunately there are two towns in France by that name so they can fight it out between themselves over which is responsible.

Blapper *noun* remote control

'The **blapper**'s covered in peanut butter.'

Jenny Rice.

Blish *noun* poor, weak tea, derived from dishwater

'There's only **blish** in the pot I'm afraid'

Kit Merrill.

Blitter *noun* remote control

'For some reason John's taken the **blitter** with him on holiday!'

Alexandra Phillips.

Blob *verb* to fail to turn up to work on time, as in **Blobbing** *present participle* failing to turn up for one's work shift at the right time

> 'I see Fred's **blobbing** again.'

Guy Gibson. If your bus doesn't arrive punctually in Derbyshire or Nottinghamshire it's probably because a driver has been blob-bing. The word stems from the 'blob', which was placed against the driver's name by the bus company timekeeper to indicate a missed shift. It is also used as an insult. A 'right blobber' is someone who's always on the blob.

Bloiky *adjective* the feeling in your stomach after you have eaten too much

> 'After the burgers, the fish 'n' chips, the Chinese and Indian take-aways and the six bags of crisps, I'm not surprised you're feeling **bloiky**.'

Charles Frederick White, whose son Marcus White created it to describe how he felt when he had eaten too much. It has now been taken up and used by the other members of the family. In view of growing obesity rates it's a word we ought to hear used more often.

Blooper-dooper *noun* remote control

> 'What made you think it was a good idea to bury the **blooper-dooper** in the Christmas pudding?'

Lud Boden.|

Bobbit *noun* a child who is unable to sit still. Can also be used as a verb

> 'I've got four children and all of them are **bobbits**.'

Linda Guest and used by eight members of her extended family.

Bocky *adjective* broken or precarious. Can also mean limping.

> 'Careful now! I think I've got a **bocky** leg.'

Anna Fenton and used in Ireland.

Boffish *adjective* muscular, self-important and not over-bright. 'Typified by prize-winning rams, bulls and head boys of minor public schools', according to the Morse family

> 'Can't stand that Simon guy. He's so **boffish**.'

Barry Morse.

Boggler *noun* remote control

> 'I'll say this for the very last time. Give me the **boggler**!'

Katharine Augarde.

DEBORAH MOGGACH
Novelist, TV and film writer

The lavatory is king!

My words are all family words which we still use.

B Square: this is our word for a bra. I can remember my mother talking to us about her B square. Its origin comes from 'B times two' – in other words, the breast times two. Something to cover up and hold up the two breasts. That's the bra or, in our family, the B square.

Butt: the TV set, not the remote control. My son, when he was very young (and this was, of course, before we had the remote control), would talk about the button to press on the television set, and call it 'the butt', which in turn became the set itself. We still use it.

Doodoos: our word for going to the toilet. You would do 'doodoos'. Again, it is a word to use instead of another more embarrassing word.

King: this is the lavatory. I'm sure it came from the phrase sitting on the throne, which I know some people use to go to the loo. It was too embarrassing to talk of the lavatory for some reason, so we called it the throne. My sister and I still use it.

As you can see, quite a few of these words we use in our family are words to cover up what we clearly thought was a more embarrassing or awkward word to say.

I suspect that's the case in many families.

Bogwurple *verb to* walk through a muddy/squelchy area

> 'So it's a choice of **bogwurpling** in Norfolk or sunbathing in the Seychelles? I'll go **bogwurpling**.'

Samuel Lesley, who says that his family uses it. 'We walked through a marshy area in East Anglia while on holiday and the word popped out of my mouth.'

Boking *noun* the sound that cats and dogs make when being sick (boke is the resultant vomit!)

> 'Did you hear Fido's **boking** last night?'

Mrs Rachel Offley. Coined by Bill Hayhurst and used for a generation by his family.

Bollay *noun* rice pudding

> 'He polished off that **bollay** pretty quickly.'

Invented by the five-year-old son of Vicky Smith and now used by three generations of the family.

Bollotics *noun* the definition is implicit in the comment, 'Generally used over breakfast when listening to a Radio 4 interview with a politician – I am sure you can understand its meaning'

> 'At least John Humphrys doesn't take any of that **bollotics**.'

T Whatley.

See also: **testiculate**

Bomper *noun* remote control

'I put the **bomper** under the table leg to keep it steady.'

Laura Woods, who comments: 'My entire family uses it. Our old TV made a noise that sounded like "bomp" when you changed the channel.' Sounds like channel-surfing on a tea-tray.

Bongogobble *noun* sales talk used for 'drumming up new business'

'Right, team. It's time for some serious **bongogobble**.'

Simon Rose of Cellar Seal, and used by his staff. It may sound like mumbo-jumbo to you but bongogobble is the Viagra of the sales pitch.

Boom Boom *noun* remote control

'Right, it's **boom boom** time.'

Claire Padel, who recalls of the McSorley family, 'My father used to watch the Basil Brush programme with his granddaughter Jessica Willans on his knee. He always had possession of the remote and would signal to her that the programme was about to begin by flourishing the boom boom, and this became one of her earliest words.'

Boomting *adjective* very good-looking in a sexy way

'Wow! He's so **boomting**!'

Heather Dooley and her mates.

Boop *noun* eccentric or 'nutty' person as described by sales staff in Wales

> 'Did you see the **boop** who bought that pair of zebra socks?'

Graham Plant.

Boselda *noun* means a 'good fellow' in some parts of the Yorkshire-Lincolnshire borderlands and also, perhaps, in the merchant navy

> 'You know Steve? I think he's a **boselda**.'

The Carpenter and Le Gras families.

Boshi *adjective* describes a rough sea crashing on to the beach because it 'sounds like the waves'

> 'The sea's been very **boshi** today.'

The Cutler family.

Britoid *adjective* something non-British but displaying a British influence when seen abroad

> 'The lawn of that *gîte* looks very **britoid**.'

Philip Kwan.

Broink *adjective* poor-quality

'Don't go to that restaurant – it's completely **broink**.'

The Field family.

Brizzles *adjective* the feel of a wool sweater when worn on bare skin

'Do you like feeling **brizzles**?'

Ron Robinson. Used first in Canada by Ron's baby brother ('a sensitive soul') when he wore a sweater without a shirt or T-shirt underneath. Now used by Tim, Ron and Jack.

Buccapedium *noun* used by the well-educated, middle-class folk of Surrey when summoning up their Latin to explain they've been tactless. 'Opening one's big mouth and putting one's foot in it or Foot-in-mouth disease'

'Arriving in Guildford I bumped into Titus and committed such a **buccapedium**!'

E White.

Bucket *verb* to accost, but normally in form **bucketed**. Apparently this happens regularly amongst the ex-pat English community in south-west Turkey and means one has been 'accosted by a loud, opinionated person who has an exaggerated sense of their own importance and disdain for those around them'

'Guess who I was **bucketed** by on the beach?'

John Hyatt.

Buffle *verb* physically to push one or more people out of the way with the body (and sometimes head as well!) or forcibly wiggle into a position in front of or between people. This word, normally as **buffling**, was originally made up by the children of the Miles family to describe what happened in skirmishes between them. However, it is now happily used by all the generations. So be careful when you visit them!

'Dad! Stop Harry. He's **buffling** again.'

Peter Miles.

Bumper *noun* remote control

'Don't hit Bill with the **bumper**.'

Daisy Mann-Peet.

Bumphled *adjective* describes clothes that are caught up with each other and not neatly on the body (for example, when your shirt sleeves are caught up under your jumper)

'You can't leave the house looking so **bumphled**.'

Angela Moreland and used by her family and friends. 'Mum and Dad have used this word since my childhood – my Brownie uniform made me look like a "sack tied in the middle" because my vest was all bumphled up under my top.' Yes, we know that feeling all too well.

Bunnage *collective noun* all forms of cake, pastry, pudding etc, also including biscuits

'What would you like from our **bunnage**?'

Gareth Williams, who says that his family uses it when 'cake or biscuit or pasty is too specific'. This may be the Mother of all Kitchen Table Lingo words.

Buppy/Bupsie *noun* a slice of bread and butter

'I'll have a **buppy** with some strawberry jam.'

Used by three generations of the McDade family. William McDade says it was 'first used by great grandmother to our toddlers and it's still used today. I'm now seventy!'

Busherise *verb* to make up a completely new word 'on the fly' or turn a noun into a verb

'Whatever the legacy at least we can **busherise**.'

Nigel Cooper and his family. 'It's derived from the tendency of George W Bush to supplement his weak command of English in this way.'

Buttonbox *noun* remote control

> 'What do I press on the **buttonbox** for *Big Brother*?'

Shirley Grove-Grayling, Sinead Longden, Robert Skelton and Wendy Weston. Sinead Longden comments: 'My sister didn't understand the words "remote control" so she just said the obvious – buttonbox.' Robert Skelton's experience was similar. 'In 1982 after I had purchased my first video recorder, remote controls were fairly new to the market. Being young, I looked at the remote control and thought it looks like a box full of buttons, hence the term buttonbox.'

Buzzy *noun* vacuum cleaner

> 'After that party we'll need a new **buzzy**.'

Sandra Parrett, who explains 'When my husband was young, he couldn't describe his mother's vacuum cleaner, so he used to call the vacuum a "buzzy" from the noise it made. It is pronounced with a flat "u" as in wuzzy.' It is now used by both sides of the family.

Add your own KTL word here

word

definition

sample

The tragedy of the **aganauts**

'Right team, **arker** to me. It's time for some serious bongogobble. We just have to *asqueviate* to the **aggranoyous** environmental lot and find a way of selling more Agas or we will go bust. It's not as if this situation has bejoisted on us. But at the moment we're just bimbling along.'

Charles looked up at his motley sales force. There was Davina, so **boomting** that it was easy to get distracted. Then Spencer, truly a *boselda* and just the kind of person you needed in a crisis. And finally Tim, **boop** with those ridiculous zebra socks and as always wearing his perpetual boffish grin.

'The market's in a real **cafoodle**. To be honest with you, I wake up every morning and just want to shout **Birkenhead, Birkenhead, Birkenhead**. We simply have to do something about this or we'll all be out of a job. It's an **accifault**.

'You'll be pleased to know that I have a cunning plan to defeat those **babobs** of the green movement. We're going to make a new kind of Aga that is so **beans** it will make all those aganauts feel that they have really arrived.

'All new Agas from now on will be run on electricity generated from kitchen waste. Think of it! The ovens will actually work and it will be possible to turn the whole thing off when you are not using it. It's just **avlexly**! I don't know why we haven't thought of it before. It'll be a *biggoron* to convert them all but I know we can do it. You lot just need to get out there and berwyn away. No need to be **cafustulated** anymore. Put on your most **cakey** look and sell, sell sell!

'This will go down as the most *bedooftey* sales strategy ever. What do you think?'

C

Cafoodle *noun* a proper mess or mix-up applied to situations or people but not to untidy rooms or messy things

'That's another fine **cafoodle** you've got us into.'

Alison Rundle and her family, going back to her granny, 'possibly because it sounds like muddle'.

Cafustulated *adjective* confused, anxious, mixed up and beside oneself – a childlike confusion

'Now he's older it's sad the way he gets so **cafustulated** by modern life.'

Debbie Edge. Created by her sister, Jackie, when she was younger and sounds like what it is!

Cakey *adjective* someone who is rather inane, insincere and over-polite

'Don't you just hate the way she looks at you? She's so **cakey**.'

Used by Ian Mackenzie and his extended family in Devon.

Cajunka *noun* remote control

'Chuck me the **cajunka**!'

Brenda Smith and family.

Capudgel *noun* the technical term for fluff

'My pockets are full of **capudgel**.'

Dan and friends.

Cav *abbreviation* 'Can I have?' Also **Caniva**, as in 'Can I have a . . .?'

'**Cav** a go?'

A shorthand for Susan Ashmead and her family.

Chainsaw *noun* potato boiled then deep-fried to produce quick roast potatoes

'These **chainsaws** are melt-in-the-mouth delicious.'

Chris Cussen, named after a Scottish friend who gave him the recipe and whose nickname was Chainsaw (from a Billy Connolly sketch).

Channel changer *noun* remote control

'Quick, pass me the **channel changer**, please.'

Robin Pitt and John Patten.

Channel-panel *noun* remote control

'Who's got the **channel-panel**?'

Dylan Morgan and family.

Charlie Blablee *noun* someone blamed for everything that goes wrong, also spelt **Blabley**

> '**Charlie Blablee** did it!'

Anna Cavill. First used in Dorset by her brother (when small) to cast the blame on others.

....

Chewdameggis *noun* very thick black hair on arms, legs and chests

> 'Wow! That's a forest of **chewdameggis** you have on your chest!'

Mark Tomlinson, who thinks it may have been first used about an uncle with particularly thick hair on his arms and chest by him and his sister and then adopted by the family.

....

Chig *noun* the bit left on a fruit or vegetable that originally connected it to the plant

> 'Before you cut up the fruit, don't forget to remove the **chigs**.'

Philip Owen and family in Lancashire.

....

Chimper *noun* small remote control used for opening automatic garage doors or unlocking car central locking remote but not for the TV remote!

> 'Where's my **chimper** got to?'

Simon Fletcher and his friends Drew Jon and Fay use it, especially when they need to ask for help in finding it.

Chickens *collective noun* the bits of hair that stick up first thing in the morning

> 'Don't forget to comb your hair. Your **chickens** look very silly.'

Caroline Challis.

Chipele *adjective* cheap and nasty

> 'Those shoes look so **chipele**!'

Honey Lucas, as used by her mother and the rest of the family.

Chobble 1. *adjective* anything that looks as if it has been chewed by mice 2. *verb* to chew noisily (especially used in the Black Country by those born in the 1940s) 3. *noun* as in a **chobbler**, a specific word for a garden shredder

> 'Stop **chobbling**, I can't hear myself think.'

Jennifer Payne, Simon Bennett and Fay Andrews all use this word but in very different ways!

Chong *verb* to cut a large slice of cake to a more manageable size, usually by cutting it across, to enable it to be picked up with the fingers. The word describes the action of cutting.

> '**Chong** me one more piece please!'

Ken Beckett says that rather than ask for the person who is cutting the cake to cut it into smaller pieces they'd asked him or her to chong it.

Chopsin *noun* when two people are nagging one another

> 'I wish you two would stop your **chopsin**!'

Sandra Parrett: 'Many years ago, when we were first married, we were bickering in the kitchen when my mother-in-law suddenly said "I wish you two would stop your chopsin!"'

....

Chuckalooloo *noun* a well-loved child of any age but especially a young child

> 'Come along, my little **chuckalooloo**.'

Judith Johnson. Used by parents but only to their own children.

....

Chumpy *adjective* really good or happy, e.g. 'That's chumpy!' or just 'Chumpy!'

> 'I feel so **chumpy** today!'

Bruce Duthie, and widely used in his family. 'The younger of my two nephews started using this word a couple of years ago. He was asked where it came from but he didn't know. Subsequently, it has fallen into use within the family – it just sounded right I suppose!'

....

Chupley *noun* a cup of tea

> 'I could murder a **chupley**'

Celia Townsend. 'A "cup of tea", morphed into a "chuppa chee" for a few months and then morphed again into "chupley". We have now used "chupley" for a cup of tea for about five years. A "chupley" is made using a chupleymatic".' (Or kettle to you and me!)

Chutchy *adjective* cute and plump, as in 'a chutchy bottom'

> 'That looks so **chutchy**.'

Raymond Buckley.

Clam *noun* a fool or idiot

> 'He's such a **clam**.'

Ann Fenton and her family in Kerry.

Clawken *adjective* feeling tired and exhausted for no particular reason

> 'I just feel so **clawken**.'

Elizabeth Smyth: 'My sisters Penny and Dee were always inventing games and words when they were very little; this one is regularly used amongst all five sisters.'

Climpers *noun* kitchen tongs, insect mouthparts, tiny fingers, etc

> 'Hold still and I'll see if I can use the **climpers** to get it out.'

Peggy-Ann Courtman: 'Our family are ancient fans of Stanley Unwin and are forever inventing words on the spur of the moment.'

Clitorati *collective noun* group of women who feel they are inherently superior to men, also used specifically to describe gay women (approvingly) as in glitterati, the fashion icons, lovely people . . .

'She's definitely one of the **clitorati**.'

Terry Hunt and Andy Brimble, but be careful how you use this one!

....

Cockroach *verb* to rush into the bathroom or lavatory just as someone else was about to go in

'Oh no, John's **cockroached** his way in before me again!'

According to Nicholas Stanley, probably the consequence of first-hand observation of large cockroaches in Africa (or at least that's what Nicholas says!)

....

Collyfoogle *verb* to manage to do a difficult job by crafty means – a bit of clever bodging

'He's an inveterate **collyfoogler**.'

John Le Gras thinks this may be from Lincolnshire or the merchant navy.

....

Colourbetical *adjective* sorted by colour

'Put them in **colourbetical** order, please.'

'Kirk' came up with this as a result of sorting out coloured felt-tipped pens

Commander *noun* remote control

> '**Commander**, please, and make it snappy.'

Helen Todd, 'Dave' and Katie Tierney all use this.

Conbulljulate *verb* used to refer to things which go wrong as in 'West Ham **conbulljulated** (lost) again.' Also *noun*, as in 'It's just one big conbulljulation.'

> 'Don't just **conbulljulate** again.'

Kendo Nagasake, used to replace profanities when speaking in front of children, women or vicars.

Conch *noun* remote control, from the shell in *Lord of the Flies*, the person holding it having the authority to speak at council meetings

> 'I have the **conch** and I have decided that we'll watch *Newsnight*.'

Richard Lowe. Don't risk changing the channel when Richard has the conch!

Confuzzled *adjective* confused and puzzled

> 'I don't know about you but I'm feeling really **confuzzled**.'

Conor Meadows reports this as used by Year 7 boys at York House School and Lucy Ramsden uses it with her family and friends.

Connel *noun* a candle

> 'Can you light the **connels** please and pipe in the haggis.'

Used by the Gall, Boulton and Hunter families in Scotland and England because this is how candles sounds in a Scottish accent.

Cooey *noun* a small space; a nook or cranny

> 'Can you squeeze into that **cooey**?'

Rob Doran. Used by three generations of his family. 'Have always heard this being used in his family in Liverpool. When I moved to Wales no one had heard of it.'

Coopies *noun* *used in plural* chickens

> 'Have you checked that the **coopies** are shut up for the night?'

Peter Weynberg and his family and others in Suffolk. 'My grandfather was a farm labourer in Suffolk, and growing up as a young girl there I knew these creatures as "coopies" or things that lived in a chicken "coop".'

Cornish *adjective* as in **Cornish thatch** – corrugated iron used for roofing

> 'That **Cornish thatch** is so rusted it can only be a matter of time before it leaks.'

Jo Livington. Used by her grandfather when she was a child in the 1950s and used and understood by four generations of her family. 'Since my grandfather always took his holidays in Cornwall I assume it derived from observation (he was an architect).'

Cosy coat *noun* dressing gown

> 'Put your **cosy coat** on, you'll catch your death of cold!'

Fiona Mackintosh: 'Our two-year-old son (now twenty-two) did not know the correct term of dressing gown and kept asking to wear his cosy coat after his bath. The term stuck and has been used since.'

Cotty *adjective* knotted up so that it cannot be combed (applied to human hair)

> 'Can you help me, Mum? My hair's all **cotty**.'

Carol Skinner. First used by her mother. 'My mum is from Leicester originally, but the word did not exist in Sheffield where I grew up.'

Coughershmingle *exclamation* like 'bless you' when someone coughs or sneezes

> '**Coughershmingle**!'

Jill Mantel and lots of other people in the USA.

Council pop *noun* tap water

'Anyone want a lovely glass of **council pop**?'

Heather Child: 'I picked this up from a colleague at work, who got it from a friend who uses the term to make tap water sound more of an exciting drink for children.'

Crodge *noun* a random item or collection of items that do not merit storage in a specific place for a specific purpose but which may nevertheless be required for some obscure reason at some indeterminate point in the future

'Have you seen the **crodge**?'

Simon Ward and his family. 'Used by my dad, possibly from his pre-war childhood in an orphanage or from his subsequent service in the army.'

Croffle *noun* small piece of polystyrene used for packing purposes

'Oh dear. The **croffles** have gone everywhere.'

Anne Jesper and her family, dating back to the 1970s when she and her husband had a mail-order business.

Croon *noun* short spiky hair just above the back of the neck

'I just love the feel of your **croon**!'

Martin Ansell and his brothers; a 'childhood name developed between rough-housing brothers which summons up the texture and feel of short back and sides'.

Cruckles *noun* generic term for the small dry biscuits that are used in most brands of speciality cat food

'Come on Tiddles, here are your **cruckles**.'

Duncan MacKillop and other cat owners.

Cruft *verb* to construct something quickly or shoddily, like 'crafting something' but with less care and attention than a craftsman. Particularly used in the IT industry

'We don't have time to do it properly, but we could **cruft** one up by tomorrow'

Angus Foreman.

Cullyups *noun* a cup of tea

'I'm dying for a **cullyups**.'

Kate Whitworth and her husband's family in Yorkshire.

Cushy up *verb* to go home and get cosy and warm and comfortable

'I can't wait to **cushy up**.'

J Tearle. Used by her late sisters-in-law originally and now by all the family when out in the cold (maybe because cushy is a slang word for 'easy'?).

D

Dacey *adjective* the assorted clothes and accessories that are bought on holiday, usually abroad, which look ridiculous when you get them home

> 'It looked great in the Seychelles but in Southampton it's just **dacey**.'

Alys Blakeway and her extended family. 'Derived from a hindu word for "locally made" and brought back to England by my aunt, an old India hand, after the Second World War.'

Dagoom *adjective* a word used by the driver and passengers in a car to indicate that the child in the back has gone to sleep

> 'Right I'll pull in here. Uh oh – **dagoom**!'

The Abercrombie family 'No clue where it came from. It just became a family word. The driver looks in the rear-view mirror, says "dagoom" and the other occupants of the car know that the child is asleep. Still works with a thirteen-year-old!' says Matthew Abercrombie.

Decan *adjective* the state when 'you are really angry and you start being nasty to people'

> 'Don't know what's wrong with her – she's just **decan**.'

Abigail (from Nairn), who says that she, her friends and family use it because 'someone made it up' and it caught on.

Deluxe *noun* the glove compartment in a car

> 'Think I left my mobile in the **deluxe**.'

Arthur Noonan. 'The early Ford Anglia had the word deluxe written across the glove compartment and that's how we referred to it.'

....

Dibber *noun* remote control (also **dibbler**)

> 'Pass me the **dibber**, please.'

Vivien Marsden, Mikko, Peter Martin, Joanna Roberts, Rachel Croix, Natalie Dale, David Cain, Kate Smith, Nic, Liz Barber, Jeremy Williams, Kate McElligot, Kath Jones and Janet Barnett all submitted this, making it one of the most popular alternatives for the TV remote.

....

Diggle-daggle *noun* the rut made in unmetalled roads after heavy rain followed by a long patch of dry weather.

> 'Careful of the **diggle-daggles** – they're pretty deep.'

The Grant family. 'Forty years ago our family were on holiday in Norway, driving up the West Coast on a road which was mostly unmetalled. The word was created by my sister, Jeanne and has stuck,' says Alison Grant.

....

Disrevelled *adjective* the look you have on the morning after a heavy night out

> 'I can see you're right **disrevelled**.'

Jean Brodie: 'I meant to say dishevelled but the new meaning was so apt, it stuck!'

Dooball *noun* a term of abuse meaning someone who is 'silly and who acts stupidly either intentionally or unknowingly'

'That guy is such a **dooball**!'

Bill Duffy, who uses it with his business partner. So do some of his staff (the ones that aren't dooballs, that is).

Doormat *noun* a sponge cake with dried fruit, burnt at the edges and dry in texture, that can only be made edible with the addition of custard

'I can only offer you **doormat**, I'm afraid.'

Charles Rodney Sabine, who says that it was invented by Granny Sabine.

Dorleybowl *noun* a bad haircut

'Would you look at that **dorleybowl** he's got on him!'

The Poxon family. 'We were sitting in the car one day, watching people go by. We spotted a bad haircut and for no particular reason, christened it a dorleybowl!' says Stephen Poxon.

Doubler *noun* a serving of fish and chips in the village of Ferndale in the Rhondda valley

'Make mine a **doubler**.'

Philip Edwards, who guesses that it comes from having two of something (so it could be pretty adaptable).

Dredra *noun* car aerial

'A dooball snapped off my **dredra**!'

Venetia Horton, who invented it as a child, but it's now regularly receiving in the Harrison and Horton families.

Drizmal *adjective* a combination of drizzle and dismal

'I'm not going out – it's too **drizmal**.'

Andrew Best: 'This was initially a slip of the tongue but we feel it perfectly describes that type of weather and the feeling it creates.'

Dunch *noun* the aching buttocks that result from sitting motionless for a long period in a car or theatre, etc

'I've got to get up – my **dunch** is killing me!'

The Peacock family in London, but they can't get to the bottom of where it came from.

Durg *noun* cigarette

'Can I cop a **durg**?'

Dan Carpenter, who says that smokers use it as an abbreviation for durgey.

JILLY COOPER (and LEO)
Author

Of drindles, goosenecks and malligers

We both use the word **drindle** to describe in somewhat derogatory terms what is a *Guardian*-reading, earnest-looking woman, often riding a bike. I'm not sure how it came about except that the word 'dirndl' is a German peasant's skirt, which was once in vogue over here. I think our drindle might come from that. We get quite a few **drindles** even down here in Wiltshire.

Another one I like in particular is **goosenecks**. These are those high-pitched voiced men, who have a protruding Adam's apple, and are frankly always very unattractive. They are nerdy too. You see them on computers on the train going up to London. I have no idea where it came from.

Another is **maliggers**, or it may be spelt **malliggers**. Anyway, it means squawking and nasty or malign seagulls or maybe just big birds. We get them in the fields near here. They're horrible. Maybe the 'mal' bit from **maliggers** comes from 'malevolent'. I just don't know. But it has a nice sound to it.

I like words which are descriptive. You can see, hear or feel what they mean even if they are not official.

Durk *noun* easy but very time-consuming tasks

'Can't watch TV – I've got too much **durk** to do.'

Phil Davies, who recalls that it is a very useful word for describing homework – especially 'endless algebra worksheets, back in school'.

••

Add your own KTL word here

word _____

definition _____

sample _____

_____

E

Earslug *noun* bluetooth phone connection piece worn in the ear

'I'll just put my **earslug** on so I can hear you better.'

Michael Marques.

Eastwesters *noun* trousers with wide legs that flap undesirably!

'Those **eastwesters** are just so groovy!'

Angela Griffiths and her occupational therapist colleagues at Charing Cross Hospital in 1984! Perpetuated by the Kennedy Family and Angela to this day. Watch out for these linguistic fashionistas!

See also **northsouthers**

ebob *noun* a pair of nuisances

'Here come those **ebobs** again.'

The Thurlby family (where troubles come in twos!).

Ecker *noun* homework

> 'I've got so much **ecker** to do tonight I won't be able to go out.'

Sally Caird. Used in her childhood in Ireland. 'It is a short version of the exercises that you would have to do for homework. I have not found it used much in England but it was well used in Eire, and children liked the harsh, distasteful challenge of the word ecker.'

....

Elephant *noun* kitchen paper

> 'Pass me the **elephant**, please.'

Chris Collins, from the idea that sheets of kitchen roll are 'tissues for elephants'. (What do you call loo rolls, Chris?)

....

Elgeril *noun* a kitchen crockery-drainer, specifically one of those wire ones with shelves

> 'Don't bother to dry up. Just put the plates in the **elgeril**.'

Jonathan Sargent, who started using this at university (a pure example of Kitchen Table Lingo)!

....

Embuggerance *noun* an exasperating problem that hinders progress

> 'That's a bit of an **embuggerance**.'

Merilyn McCall says she invented this at the MoD during preparations for the Falklands War. Used by her friends and widely by MoD personnel. The word bravely chosen by *Discworld* author Terry Pratchett to describe the sad news that he has a rare form of Alzheimer's. Also submitted by Nick Essex, who thinks it may be a corruption of 'bugbear'.

Enpufflicated *adjective* that bleary-eyed, first-thing-in-the-morning look when you are incapable of opening your eyes even though you are technically awake

'You look really **enpufflicated**!'

Carl and Helen Wright and their family.

....

Epsep *noun* the thing you save until last from your plate of food, always the favourite item

'That **epsep** was simply delicious.'

Stephen Haywood. Invented by his children and used today by the whole family. 'This seems to be a word developed among the children when they were small and with little difference in their ages (two and a half years between the three of them). There seems to have been little parental influence in the word's development – and it remains in current use a dozen years later.' Stephen thinks it may be related to 'excepted', though it's not clear why you'd find this on your plate of food!

ALAN TITCHMARSH

Author, TV presenter and gardener

'What an extreedingly fine garden!'

Most of my words come from my childhood, which was in Yorkshire, and were used mainly within our family. We always used the word **blegging** for going blackberry-picking. I've no idea where it came from, except that it seems to be a sort of elision or corruption of the word blackberrying.

But the one I really like is **extreedingly**. I think it's mine and I use it as a word to describe something that is between extremely and exceedingly. I like it because it is such a descriptive word even if it does not officially exist. It is one of those words which I think should be in the *OED*. To me it also shows the importance of words evolving from language. It also shows how very malleable and subtle the English language is.

Another one, which I know my parents used quite a bit, was the phrase **muck clarts**. These were the grubby marks on windows. I still use it a bit.

My grandmother would call her porridge 'clarty'. But I looked it up in the dictionary and it exists, meaning sticky and dirty, so would not qualify for this book. I now use clarty to describe wet clay.

Fee-first *noun* a laundry box, ideally one that is home-made

'Put your clothes in the **fee-first**, please.'

The Lucas family. According to Esther, 'Three generations of us have used this, because as children we used to fight to see who could stand on it first to do our teeth, saying "Me first for the fee-first".'

Fifty-p *noun* a story that is long, boring and pointless; a 'shaggy dog' story

'This isn't another **fifty-p**, is it?'

Francesca Fennell, Fiona Simpson, Lucy Woodward and her student friends in Winchester, and inspired by a bafflingly complex, long and uninteresting narration of how somebody, somewhere did something very ordinary with a fifty-pence piece.

Fisky *adjective* describes the state of hair which has been wildly ruffled by the wind

'Get your comb out, you're looking **fisky**!'

Miriam Shone, who says that it was invented by her twin sisters when very small 'to describe in particular our dad's hair!' Now used by three generations of the Shone family.

Flapple *noun* a 'pull-up' nappy used towards the end of potty training when the child is only wearing a nappy at night

'OK, time to put on your **flapple**.'

Ben Sheppard says this was created to deal with a very grown-up two-year-old who decided he was too big a boy for nappies! 'To appease him at night he began to wear "flapples", which are just like pants and are most definitely not nappies.'

Flimp *noun and verb* a passenger who has not been authorised by the taxi company booking office; to flimp is the act of stealing a fare that has been issued to another driver

'You'll never guess the **flimp** I had in the back of my cab last night!'

Edward George Fish. It's been in use, apparently, in the Cardiff taxi trade 'since the year dot'. But don't bother asking for a receipt for it.

Floordrobe *noun* the place that untidy teenagers use to store their clothes

'You'll find it under the pizza box on the **floordrobe**.'

Chris Hodges, who says that parents use it 'in anecdotes when describing people or places that are untidy' (i.e. their kids and their bedrooms).

ROBERT ADAM
Architect

'Give me those fluffies!'

Robert ('Bob') Adam is one of the world's leading contemporary architects working in the classical tradition. He is already the author of a standard guide to classical architectural terms but, as he says, in his office there is constant banter based on an alternative architectural vocabulary – much of it self-coined.

'It's part of making discussions easier, lighter and more humorous. The words just pop out without thinking about it. Some of these terms are so appropriate that they quickly become standard expressions – at least within the office context.'

Amongst his favourites are **frou-frou**, meaning decoration (usually excessive) on a building, **curly wurlies** for Ionic capitals, **cabbage** for Corinthian capitals and **chunky stuff** for rustication. When it comes to the bigger scale he calls large country houses (the kind of thing he specialises in) which have a central stairwell a **doughnut** house, while a fully decorated classical building is **all fruit and nuts**. And when he goes to see clients he presents them with **fluffies** – that is, coloured presentation drawings.

The one term he wasn't aware of in his office (until he asked his staff) was being **bobbed** – to be assigned to work on a major project with him!

Floozed *adjective* when one's clothes are covered in cat hair

> 'Smudge! My best trousers are **floozed**.'

Nic Holc-Thompson, who explains that in 1998 he and his wife acquired a long-hair black and white cat called Floozie. Wherever Floozie sat she would leave a trail of hair. Even when just walking up to Nic she would swish her tail and deposit cat hairs on his clothes, particularly annoying if he was about to leave the house. 'Once she slept in the tumble drier, which was turned on, and had to be rescued and cost £200 in vet's bills plus the cost of rewashing a large volume of clothing.' So now you know!

Florrie *verb* to use or repair something that most people would throw away, e.g. scraping the last bit of jam from a pot

> 'Can you **florrie** that butter? It's only a week past its use-by date.'

Jo Williams, who says that his mother, Florence (Florrie) never threw anything away if it could possibly be used.

Flup 1. *adjective* replete. Derived from 'full-up'. 2. *adjective* slumped and fed up

> 'I've already had six burgers – I'm just **flup**.'

> 'The dog looks really **flup**.'

Lesley Voice uses it in the full-up sense (in an extreme form she can even be floppy). And the Bradley family use it to describe the dog in his basket looking hard done by after being rejected in his attempt to get them to play games or give him snacks, or when he is made to wait for a walk.

Flygasm *noun* the extreme pleasure which one derives from flying a freestyle sports kite when the wind is a perfect, smooth 6 mph

'Oooooooooh – I think I'm going to have a **flygasm**.'

Steve Tonkin, who says that 'I coined this before I found that aoxomoxoa is used for the same thing.' Just how do you pronounce that?

Folgaria *noun* glasses case

'Don't forget your **folgaria**.'

Christine Sutton, who explains that it is derived from a glasses case bought in Austria by her mother. It caught on. 'When my husband came into the family my husband thought it was a proper word.' Well, it is now.

Football *noun* a present which is more likely to be enjoyed by the donor than the recipient

'This black negligee is just a **football**.'

Andrew Higham, who says it was inspired by the story of a small boy who gave his mother a football as a present.

Frabb *verb* to fidget, fuss about, twiddle with things

'I know it's raining but do you have to **frabb** so much?'

Linda Coleman, who says it comes from her husband's family. 'His late mother used this a lot and it has remained in the family ever since. It is still used.'

Kitchen Table Lingo across the UK – where some of the words come from

Aganaut – Surrey

Anagipta – Yorkshire

Bedooftey – Derbyshire

Bist – Telford

Blob – Derbyshire

Buccapedium – Surrey

Cakey – Devon

Chig – Lancashire

Clam – Kerry, Ireland

Collyfogle – Lincolnshire

Coopies – Suffolk

Cornish thatch – Cornwall

Cosy coat – Scotland

Connel – Scotland

Cotty – Leicestershire

Doubler – Rhonda valley

Dunch – London

Ecker – Ireland

Fifty-p – Hampshire

Flimp – Cardiff

Froostin – Scotland

Geat – Newcastle

Hadgie buhdgie – Cork, Ireland

The story behind **foshel**

Foshel *noun and verb* a shovel or to shovel (for example, food into your mouth or coal into the fire). Also used in the form 'to foshel it in'.

Sometimes fresh words arrive in English because they have been brought here by new arrivals. But just as often it is because native English-speakers travel far afield in search of words to enrich the vocabulary.

Hence it was with Barry Lee-Potter's father, a geologist who spent some of his key years in the mineral-rich areas of what is now Zambia. 'The multi-tribe, multi-ethnic workforce spoke many different languages both African and European,' explains Barry, who is now a successful communications executive. 'A lingua franca emerged made up of words for simple things. Amongst these was the word **fosholo**, meaning shovel, which my father brought home. It's a great onomatopoeic word, which we adapted as **foshel** to mean shovelling food into our mouths, and was then transmuted into eating quickly.'

But that wasn't the only word brought back from the workplace to infiltrate into the Lee-Potter household. There was also **muti** – originally black magic but converted into medicine; **futi**, meaning 'more of' and **miningi** meaning 'plenty'. All of these words are still in regular usage in the various Lee-Potter households of the next generation.

Homespun

But it is not just imported words that fire up the Lee-Potters. With an aunt – now deceased – a famous journalist (the highly talented Lynda Lee-Potter), words are in the family blood. Amongst Barry's Kitchen Table Lingo, therefore, is to **nubble**, which means to stroke – usually a dog or cat – in a way which is a mix of massage and caress. Then there is the recently erected **punservatory**, so much warmer and more friendly than the boring old conservatory. (In fact, when people have engaged in a little light Kitchen Table Lingo they normally go into the **punservatory** to relax and cool down.)

Barry's brother, Guy, is also a keen collector and inventor of words, including the positively dangerous-sounding **dry-smeary**, when you clean your own car windscreen by driving close behind a lorry in the rain to pick up the spray. And the **leafer**, when the book-minded diner manages to eat without taking his or her eyes off the page.

Frangled *adjective* the feeling of being very stressed

'Ahhhhhhh! I'm just so **frangled** tonight.'

Ruth Davison: 'It is an amalgamation of frayed and jangled – the feeling of being frayed at the edges and nerves jangled. First used when coping with a young family and full-time job. It just summed up how I felt and still do from time to time.' Ruth's husband, a civil servant, has been known to use it in Whitehall. Well, not surprising really.

Frarp *verb* to scratch in an unladylike way

'If you wish to **frarp** then please do it in private.'

Kim Lewis: 'Originated by my grandmother and her sisters to describe the unladylike scratch you could enjoy after taking your stays or girdle off! It was carried on by my mum into my childhood and family vocabulary.'

Fringle *adjective* disparaging term often used in conjunction with 'face'. It means that you are an idiot. Mainly used to tell people that the comment they have just made was extremely stupid

'You're such a **fringle** face.'

Amy Richardson, who gave a long account – a fifty-p (see page 50) – of how it was derived by her friends Sophie and Becky in Warwickshire from 'For English' and then applied as an insult to a boyfriend. A touch of Shakespeare here, maybe? (Erm, probably not.)

Froostin *adjective* really hot

'I'm **froostin**!'

Hazel: 'From the word "roasting", except we changed it to give it some attitude!'

. . . .

Add your own KTL word here

word _____

definition _____

sample _____

_____

HUNTER DAVIES
(AND MARGARET FOSTER)
Author and biographer

'Look at that gadjy begging for scran. How shanning for him.'

There are quite a few words which I picked up at school in Carlisle or with my family. One is **gadjy**, or at least that's how I think it is spelt. It sounds and looks a bit Indian, but I don't think it is. We'd use it to describe an old man, somebody we didn't know. Like some anonymous man on a street corner.

Another Carlisle one is **scran**, which we used for the word food. We'd say something like, 'When are you off for your **scran**?' and we'd talk at school about school **scran**. Again, I have no idea how it came about.

Yet another was **shan** or sometimes **shanned**. It meant 'embarrass'. So, to be shanned was to be embarrassed by somebody or something. You could also **shan** somebody. And it was a noun, too. That meant an embarrassing moment.

Margaret my wife also uses all three of these words. Also our eldest child, who has spent most of his life in London, knows and recognises them, but he does not use them. I don't know if they are still used in Carlisle. We have a house in the Lake District – some way from Carlisle itself – and the words are not used there, or at least I've not heard them used.

G

Gavver *noun* policeman

'Quick. Leg it. The **gavvers** are coming.'

Jade Cook says her 'chavvie mates told me it!'

Gazinta *abbreviation* a factor (in maths)

'Four **gazinta** (goes into) twenty five times.'

Steve Tonkin and his pupils. Four gazinta (goes into) twenty five times, geddit? 'It's easier to remember than "factor",' Steve says. 'A factor is a gazinta.'

Geat *adjective* very

'Your hair is **geat** lush today.'

Katie Smith and her friends in Newcastle.

Gheeney *adjective* a derogatory term for any poor, scruffy, snotty person

'Gareth's a right **gheeney**'

Gareth Hughes explains: 'In the early 1970s, there was a poor kid whose family could not afford new clothes, and he had a perpetu?ally runny nose. We used to call him Gheeney. I recently heard schoolkids on a bus in Peterborough refer to another as a right gheeney. My brothers also still use the term.'

Gidder *noun* elderly person

> 'Drive carefully, **gidders** crossing!'

John Williams.

Giffum *noun* garden gnome

> 'Don't those **giffums** look so . . . naff?'

Dan White and his extended family and some friends use it. He maintains it was what his son called garden gnomes as a baby, derived from his attempt at saying Father Christmas, which is what he thought they were. (Go to Dan's garden and you're sure of a big surprise!)

Giggage *noun* amount of hard drive space on a computer

> 'Wow. That's what I call some serious **giggage**.'

Andrea Harvey and her family.

Giggly-bit *noun* the tough, chewy pieces of fat and gristle found in cooked meat, particularly beef

> 'I am afraid I couldn't eat the **giggly-bits**.'

Laurie Pott: 'When our daughter, Christina – now aged twenty-five and working as a chef – was very young and inarticulate she literally could not bring herself to eat these bits of meat. When asked why not, she could only reply: "They just taste giggly." Hence giggly-bits.'

Gimantic *adjective* of extremely large size

> 'That's **gimantic**!'

Stewart Kempster: 'Invented by my granddaughter Emily Cracknell when aged four and derived from enormous, gigantic and ginormous.'

Gizzer *noun* waste disposal unit in kitchen

> 'Switch on the **gizzer**, please.'

Hilary Derby, whose family started to use gizmo to describe it, but this was then changed to gizzer.

Gleehueham *adjective* describes feelings associated with the morning of a day when there will be a big family gathering. All the weather conditions suggest a perfect day, and the atmosphere generated by both the climate and the people is full of glee.

> 'It's a **gleehueham** day.'

R Moorhouse and three generations of the Moorhouse family and their friends. 'First used in Byrness December 2006 when Christmas was celebrated three weeks early, as this was the only time all the family could meet up. The weather was cold but with strong winter sunshine and the ground was covered with a white frost. This was the first gleehueham day.'

Gleg *verb* to smile in a way that shows a wide expanse of very white teeth

'Here's another picture of Bill Clinton **glegging**.'

Hilary Williams. Used by the Barnes family in Coventry, originally to describe American politicians, then related to a particular kind of smile. Possibly Nottingham slang?

Gloobies *noun* gloves

'What a gorgeous pair of **gloobies**.'

Jean Howell and her family.

Glumpy *adjective* gloomy, dull or overcast day

'Another **glumpy** day.'

K D Tubby.

Gnome *noun* a favour done or item purchased for someone living abroad

> 'When you go back to the UK could you buy me one of those **gnomes**?'

Rosemary Grave. Used by her friends, especially those who live or have lived abroad. 'A South African friend, departing for a tour of Europe, asked me to purchase garden gnome moulds for her mother in Cape Town.' And the name stuck. Make sure they don't come back with a giffum!

Gobies *adjective* feeling dreadful

> 'I'm feeling **gobies**.'

Karin Elmberg, in some way (not explained!) to do with the Gobi Desert!

Golden *verb* to grow old gracefully

> 'She's **goldening** so gracefully, don't you think?'

Kathy Maas and her family use this in the USA. She tells us that 'it's a spin-off of the word olding (coined by my then seven-year-old son, and meaning turning older).'

Gongle *verb* (of dogs) to gnaw at a large bone

> 'He's going at it like a dog **gongling** a bone.'

Anthony Glanville, whose family have used this for a long while to describe the way dogs gnaw at large bones. Pleasingly descriptive and might also be a handy way of describing how some people eat, too!

Gooter *noun* any improvised, hand-held tool, like a brush-head on the end of a flexible wire for digging dirt out of hard-to-reach places or a hooked piece of metal for getting paint-tin lids off

> 'This is just the kind of job for a **gooter**.'

Esmee Rust and her four siblings. 'My elder sister used the word when she was young to describe any tool she did not know the name of, and the word still retains this second meaning.'

Grananat *noun* dressing gown

> 'Mr Rowell, you do look smart in that little **grananat**!'

Sue Rowell, whose small son called it that when he received a new dressing gown aged three (he's now eighteen).

See also **cosy coat**

Granernity *noun* a grandparent taking time off work to help care for a newborn grandchild

> 'Thank goodness Mum was able to take **granernity** leave and look after Tom.'

Judy Rodier, herself a grandparent and her family. 'If you have maternity and paternity leave, it stands to reason that you can have granernity leave.'

Grendle *verb* to break something up into small pieces

> 'Give me the cake and I'll **grendle** it.'

Edward Gall and his circle of friends.

Griffley *adjective* somewhere between mischievous and grumpy in temperament and/or appearance

'See you're in a **griffley** mood this morning.'

Chris Cardell-Williams. Originally coined as a description of certain dogs, this has become generally descriptive of an argumentative nature with mischievous intent, animal or human.

Grinkling *adjective* a cross between grizzling and whimpering

'Ssshhh! Please don't wake her up. She's really **grinkling** this morning.'

Malka Baker. Especially used to describe a child when s/he is not very content.

Groggled *adjective* damaged

'Don't use that one, it's **groggled**.'

Yvonne, whose father first used it when the cat damaged our sofa.

Grooglum *noun* a small leftover item, usually wet; for example, the bits of porridge left in the sink after washing the pot

'Who did the washing up? You've left all the **grooglums** in the sink.'

Andrew Whiteside, who says it is just one of many words that his late father coined when they were growing up.

Growbert *noun* a child who is going through a rapid increase in stature

> 'Ben's a real **growbert** at the moment.'

Alan Dagnall, after overhearing a conversation 'in which somebody commented that his brother Jack was having a growth spurt'.

Gruds *noun* (also **grunts**) underpants

> 'Someone's left their **gruds**, or should I say **grunts**, on the kitchen floor.'

Mof Gimmers explains that it's used by the people of Horwich in the north-west. 'It's derivative of Grunderpants, but alas, I know no more.'

Guffy *adjective* being cheeky to your elders or those of more senior rank

> 'He's so **guffy**.'

Alice McLuskie and her father's parents used the word. 'I believe it may have been naval slang, and certainly my grand?father and my grandmother's father and three brothers were all naval officers.'

Gum gum *noun* remote control

> 'My hands are glued to the **gum gum**.'

Cynthia Wan, whose family and boyfriend use the word, explains: 'Gum means push a button or press in Cantonese. However, we use this word in otherwise English sentences.'

Gwaggle 1. *verb* to dither 2. *adjective* (**gwaggly**) feeling uncertain, and also to feel as though one might be about to be sick 3. *plural noun* (**gwaggles**) severe diarrhoea

> 'Be with you in a moment. Got a terrible attack of the **gwaggles**.'

Maria James: 'The origin of the word is probably from our mother. She speaks four languages fluently, and has no difficulty inventing words and entire rules of grammar to suit her needs!' Just hope she knows when to gwaggle and when not to.

Add your own KTL word here

word _____

definition _____

sample _____

_____

H

Hadgie buhdgie *adjective* fast asleep, as used in Waterford, Ireland

> 'I was **hadgie buhdgie** under a hedge when this cow woke me up.'

Anna Fenton and her family.

Hammershaft *exclamation* an expression of surprise

> 'What the **hammershaft**! Oh, another one of yours, I see.'

Mr R Burnley, whose grandfather exclaimed, 'What the hammershaft?' when he unexpectedly sat on a wooden toy left on his armchair by a child. The family have used it ever since.

Hauntler *noun* stuffed and mounted stag's head (normally staring down balefully from the walls of gloomy baronial halls)

> 'Why are those **hauntlers**' eyes staring at me?'

Michael Elliott, who comments: 'Years ago, one of our children became frightened for no apparent reason whilst we were visiting a stately home. Later, when asked about this, she said "It was the hauntlers, Mummy." Since then, mounted game trophies have always been "hauntlers" in our family.' (Perhaps they frighten the ghosts too.)

The story behind **harfer**

Harfer *verb* to breathe in a confined space, especially a car, causing condensation to collect on the windows

John Hamer was astonished when he used the word harfer to describe the misting up of the windows of his car but no one else understood what it meant. 'I thought it was in common use but it turned out to be just my family.

'I think it was my dad, Jim, who invented it because it reminded him of the heavy breathing of people he had known.' The people he had particularly in mind were older family members who had suffered from the illnesses that were commonplace in the industrial northern cities. As many were the victims of asbestosis and asthma the sound of hoarse, heavy breathing was familiar. It required only a short migration to apply it to breathing very heavily so as to create condensation. It has now moved on to a third generation of users. His nephew and niece now use harfer too.

Love those words

Other words, too, have come down through the family – such as **pudgers** for children – and, of course, there is a family word for the remote control, namely the **spizzer**. John is concerned, though, that the pressures of mass culture – especially the American influence – may be having a homogenising effect on the language at large. 'I'm a real word lover and I encourage people to be interested and inventive with words.'

One continuing source of new language, says John, is the world of pop music. So long as the young stay creative the wells of new language should continue to gush.

Hearthstone Edge *noun* indicates (in north Manchester) that you are staying at home for your holiday

> 'Going to **Hearthstone Edge** for your holidays again this year?'

Brian Hoy, who explains its provenance as 'the front of a coal fireplace. This means not leaving home at all!' An ideal destin?ation, then, if you are suffering from the credit crunch.

Helene *noun* leftovers that are put into the fridge even though everyone knows that they will probably not be used and will eventually be thrown out

> 'There's nothing to eat except **helene** from Sunday.'

John Russell, who explains that he and his extended family use it, having been inspired by a former flatmate, called Helene, who refused to put any leftovers in the fridge because she was convinced – probably correctly – that they would all be thrown out eventually. (Of course, nowadays no one would be so wasteful.)

Hench *adjective* well built, well muscled, well toned

> 'Don't mess with my boyfriend. He's **hench**.'

Several contributors, including Natasha Fegan, Connor Stanhope and Henry Dorling from Basingstoke who comments: 'As a teacher I have noticed this word being used in day-to-day class-room discussion between students referring to people they have come across in the gym or in their social circles. Not exactly sure from where it derives from, but it is a sort of "street" lingo.' One suggestion is that it comes from 'Henchman', i.e. the muscular, but possibly stupid, sidekick.

Herm-afro-dite *noun* a person with a sexy afro hairstyle

> 'I want my sweet **Herm-afro-dite**, I'll hold her close, throughout the night.'

Dan, who says that Sam and her friends ('including me') use it when talking with friends about 'our ideal boy or girlfriends'.

Himp *noun* an awkward lump or ruffle in clothing, particularly socks

> 'I was hobbling down the street because of this **himp**.'

Kathryn Douglas, who explains that at age four her son Lawrence created the word due to his frustration at having lumps in his socks in uncomfortable places. It has subsequently been used by the whole family – Lawrence, Tayla, Kathryn and Mark Douglas plus all nannies and grandads too! – to describe various ruffles and lumps in clothing which make them uncomfortable or distorted. Sounds like most haute couture.

Hodderduh *noun* a carpet-sweeper or a hand-propelled lawnmower

> 'I don't care if it's eco-friendly – it's time we got rid of that **hodderduh**.'

Sarah Johnson, who says that she and her friends use it having been inspired by 'an Eddie Izzard stand-up routine when he is describing the noise made by a carpet-sweeper/hand-propelled lawn mower'. So you can cut the carpet with it or clean up the lawn.

Hodgey *adjective* disgruntled, miserable, out of sorts, short-tempered

> 'He didn't get back from the pub until half two. No wonder she's **hodgey**.'

John R Corsan. Normally applied in the Corsan family to people who arrive at the breakfast table having had a bad night, although John is not sure which family member actually invented it. Typical Kitchen Table Lingo really – suddenly it's just there and everyone's using it.

Hoog *adjective* to be cool in a hippy way

> 'That hat is so **hoog**.'

Debbie Private: 'My nine-year-old son made it up about a year ago. Now we all use it. The word is pronounced phonetically as hooj.' So it's kind of Woodstock crossed with Glasto.

Hookum *noun* an activity, usually involving a journey, which is undertaken by more people than are strictly necessary for the task

> 'Why did three of you go to London? Sounds like an expensive **hookum** to me.'

Charles Rodney Sabine.

Hork *expletive* an expression of disgust which can also be shouted as an exclamation. (May be helpful as a four-letter word you can use in polite company). Also takes the adjectival form of horky, meaning unpleasant or, at best, naff.

> 'Oh **hork**! **Hork**! **Hork**! I cannot believe it!'

Gloria McShane, who comes originally from Ontario, Canada, where her birth family use it. Her British husband and children have now adopted it too.

....

Horserubbish *noun* a synonym for horseradish

'Please pass the **horserubbish**.'

Anne Atkins, who says, 'I think it was Frank Muir who said – on the radio – that this was what he called it.' Any road, it's now in regular use in the Atkins family.

....

Howzit *interrogative* how are you?

'**Howzit**, Mr Mugabe?'

Patricia Thompson, who says it is common among English-speaking South Africans and Zimbabweans.

....

Humsecker *noun* the double-ended oven glove which hangs from the rail of a kitchen stove

'Where's the **humsecker** gone? I need to get that joint out.'

Michael Hills, who observes that thirty people of three generations of his family now use it (although presumably not all at the same time).

The story behind **hoogelly**

Hoogelly *adjective* describes something between cosy, charming and pleasant

There are already many hundreds of words with Danish origins in the English language, but Elizabeth Hojlund and her family have added one more with the creation of hoogelly. 'I married a Dane and found the Danish loved parties and social events which were friendly, warm and cosy. They had a word for this, which we adapted as hoogelly. But the point is that it has much wider application than just cosy. For example, you can have a hoogelly meeting or regard a person as hoogelly in a way that the word cosy would not be right. It's really an all-purpose word which can mean gentle and pleasant as well.'

An answer to the cold

The Hojlund family has a habit of adopting foreign words and phrases into their personal vocabulary – for example, they use a number of Spanish words between themselves – but hoogelly is the only one that they now regard as being properly anglicised. They feel that it is filling a gap in English, although they recognise that the Danish conditions that gave rise to Hoogelly are not directly transferable.

'Because the winters are cold and long in Denmark the Danes go out of their way to soften the cold and brighten things up. They use lots of little candles and make an effort with delicious food to make things as pleasant as possible. All of that is hoogelly.'

Maybe there is something the British could learn from this?

I

Improposition *noun* 1. an invitation to someone to have illicit sex 2. an invitation to someone to have sex otherwise than in the missionary position

'Fancy an **improposition** from me?'

Keith Patchett (who hopes that nobody is offended by his linguistic creativity!).

Init *noun* holidaymaker word used by locals as result of hearing them say 'init nice here'

'It must be summertime. Winchester is seething with **inits**.'

Michael Wilkins.

Intertwingle *verb* to describe two or more concepts or objects that are totally entwined and interdependent so that they form a new meaning

'Dithering and government have become quite **intertwingled** in my mind'

Helen Renwick. Used by Madeleine Willis and her friends working in universities where concepts often mix together.

Irwins *noun* crocodile forceps (a medical instrument)

> 'Make sure the **irwins** are in place before I check the crocodile's teeth.'

Christian Hughes and staff at Fivelands veterinary centre in Birmingham. 'Named after Steve Irwin the Australian TV presenter who used to do dangerous things with crocodiles. He was a bit of a hero with the staff at our veterinary practice, and the name was awarded posthumously.'

··

Ish *noun* shoe

> 'How many **ishes** did you say you wanted me to buy Imelda?'

Penny Carter and her family use this word. (Her mother and aunt used the word when they were children.)

The story behind **Jargoon Harry**

Jargoon *noun* large pimple or boil on face normally used in phrase 'jargoon Harrys'

Leila Levine's dad was so full of invented words and wordplay that she can barely remember a fraction of it. He was an East Ender of the old school. He took his holidays on Canvey Island and had a vocabulary that drew on a rich soup of language. The main ingredient may have been traditional cockney 'backslang', but it also contained many other ingredients – including Yiddish, Russian and a range of the other linguistic influences that descended on the great port of London.

So when he described as jargoon Harrys those of Leila's schoolgirl friends who had the misfortune to have spots and pimples it was just part of the regular mix of unusual and non-standard words which flowed around the house. 'It wasn't intended as insulting or rude, it was just the way he spoke all the time. And as I had quite a number of friends who had spots at that age it was used quite a lot.'

A culture of jollity

Amongst his older male friends and workmates Leila's father had a vocabulary which she suspects was 'mostly vulgar' but that didn't come into the home, where he was 'very protective' of his daughter. But Leila thinks that having a rich and varied language was symptomatic of a general 'culture of jollity'. She looks now at the rap generation and sees them as having the a similar kind of freedom that allows inventiveness and creativity with the language as her father's.

By contrast, Leila herself has not been so prolific with new words – something she blames on having been through the rigours of the academic system. 'It's very stultifying to have done an English degree,' she says. 'It keeps you on the straight and narrow.' Not that this has stopped the family words of her dad passing through the generations. 'My daughter is in America and she has taken jargoon over there, where it is also now being used.'

J

Jackpot *noun* the sound a jackdaw makes in the chimney pot

> 'It's the **jackpot**.'

Yvonne Goodes, whose mother, when under pressure, accidentally shortened the sentence 'The jackdaw's in the chimney pot.' It stuck fast to describe the noise the bird makes.

Jahmean/Jamean *interrogative* 'Do you know what I mean?'

> 'Wha' **jahmean** (**jamean**)?'

Ian Andrews (jahmean) and Karen McIntosh (jamean) who adds: 'My friend Si is in a league of his own when it comes to speaking the English language, and he has a tendency to shorten words and phrases to suit. For example "seriously" has become "Seesly".' Sounds like an oral version of txtg.

Jamesilated *verb* to be destroyed by a younger sibling

> 'I see the car's just been **jamesilated**.'

Katie Walling (and long-suffering family), who comments: 'I have a brother named James who used to destroy everything.'

Jampot *verb* the action of a cat putting its leg in the air when it cleans itself

> 'Preppy's at the bottom of the garden **jampotting**.'

Angie Mcgeown and the other five members of her family, who say that it was inspired by 'the appearance of the cat'. We'll leave this to your imagination.

....

Jar tub *noun* kitchen sink

> 'Just put them all in the **jar tub**.'

Colin Campbell and his family.

....

Jewl/Jewel *adjective* an expression of support and appreciation equivalent to 'great'. Very popular, apparently, in Leicester

> 'That Gary Lineker's **jewl**, isn't he!'

Kamal Joshi: 'I have no idea of the derivation. I heard it one day, and at first I hated it but then I found myself using it.'

....

Jifficate *adjective* to clean items in the house

> 'OK, I think it's Tony's turn to **jifficate**.'

Tony Ginman and his family who get it all done, we're sure, in just a jiffy.

Jollop *verb* to go out somewhere to enjoy oneself

'Can we afford to **jollop** today?'

Derek Alexander and family, who say it comes from the word 'jolly' and was in use at least thirty years ago. Ah, those were the days.

Jigger muffin *noun* a naughty child

'Wait until I get my hands on that **jigger muffin**.'

Nigel Watson, who explains: 'On holiday my younger children were being very loud and annoying. In exasperation I called them a bunch of jigger muffins.' The whys and wherefores are lost in time.

Jiggy joggy *noun* the gallops (for racing horses) according to locals in Downton, Wiltshire

'I've just taken the old nag out to the **jiggy joggy**.'

Yvonne Goodes.

Jiggypoo *noun* a tool or technical item whose name temporarily escapes you

'Tell you what – I'll lend you my **jiggypoo**.'

Bernard A Smith, who uses it along with his friends and work-mates. It was exported by Bernard's sister from Canada, where it is used extensively (no doubt, because the country has a large and thriving jiggypoo industry).

The story behind **jojo**

Jojo *noun* (pronounced joe-joe) novice, or a person who does most things incorrectly or foolishly (which usually ends in tears – or at least tears of laughter)

Kitchen Table Lingo is to be found everywhere that English is spoken and not least in Africa, where it is predominantly the language of business and technology. One of the favourite words that Charles Megafu uses is **jojo**. 'There are characters which people exhibit sometimes that makes one wonder what could be responsible for that kind of thing,' says Charles. 'And there are times when the human mind goes blank and a person finds himself doing things in an unusual way. For example, like blowing off a light bulb instead of switching it off. To do that is to behave like a **jojo**. He's a person who does most things incorrectly – such as roasting the egg instead of frying it.'

Jojo the outsider

Jojo can also be applied to a new member of a group, clique or organisation when he has not yet become an insider. 'He can be called a **jojo** because he is not yet used to the words which are commonly used by the group or he is not yet accustomed to their way of doing things.'

Charles says that **jojo** was first coined in 2006 in the Oaknet Cyber Café in Onitsha (Anambra State, Nigeria), where he used to work. 'It is now used in my family, in my new office where I work, in social gatherings and in neighbouring towns close to Onitsha.' Beyond that, Charles suspects it has also been carried into other states including Lagos and Port Harcourt.

Another KTL word Charles mentions is **maga**. This describes the victims of internet fraud (either by collecting money from the person or information). So maybe it's marginally better to be a **jojo** than a **maga**!

JRR Tolkien *verb* talking

> 'Now you're **JRR Tolkien**.'

The Galls, Boultons and Hunters who live in Darlington, where presumably English is a second language to Elvish.

Juckler *noun* a dog

> 'I think pikeys walking their **jucklers** look so sweet.'

'Tom', who merely says that it's used by pikeys in Newark. If anyone is offended by this – whether pikeys, dogs or even residents of Newark – we profoundly apologise. But it seemed too good to leave out.

Justin *noun* someone who turns up with, for example, dirty cups and plates just before the washer-upper empties the sink

> 'I was just about to dry my hands when half a dozen **justins** turned up.'

Valerie Cook who, along with her family members, was constantly saying 'just in time' to the late arrivals. As a result anyone turning up at the last moment is now referred to as Justin.

Add your own KTL words here

word _____

definition _____

sample _____

_____

word _____

definition _____

sample _____

_____

word _____

definition _____

sample _____

_____

SIMON ARMITAGE

Poet, novelist and playwright

Remember the jozzers and the jozzerettes?

Language must evolve as nobody owns it. New spoken language has a very fast turnover. And language in Britain is also very tribal – among groups, a school class or a gang. We benefit hugely from being able to communicate through our constantly moving language. Here are some of my words.

Gumby: it's a noun that we used at school to describe somebody whose jaw stuck out – the opposite of the chinless wonder. It was a term of abuse to describe the sort of boy who we thought was an idiot.

Jozzer: another secondary school word from the 1980s and was, I suppose, the 'chav' of that era. It meant a lad who was naughty, who didn't turn up for lessons. But then we also had the word 'jozzerines' for the bad girls, and even 'jozzerettes' for the very young bad kids.

Seemeon: this is a noun that our family has used for at least two or three generations. It means a 'snack', and I think it must have come about as something to 'see me on' until lunch or dinner. In other words, the three words have been elided.

Rism: another noun in use in our family. It describes the smallest amount – like an iota. We would use it in the context of there not being 'a rism of truth' in something. No idea where it comes from.

Ninasimone: now this comes from the singer Nina Simone. It describes the cream you buy or the spray for mosquito bites when you are abroad. I know it actually comes from the word 'Neosayomol', which is the name of the cream we first bought in Spain for the bites. With not so good pronunciation it became Ninasimone.

Holmfirthing: this comes from a village near us called Holmfirth. It's been used for generations to describe somebody who we think cheats or we don't like. It's a put-down because, to be frank, the people in Holmfirth have always had a bit more money so we were envious of them. Hence our put-down.

K

Kafka *adjective* a description of how you're feeling or how your day has gone when everything is going wrong. Or just a general exclamation of anger

'How are you?'

'To be honest I'm feeling pretty **kafka**.'

Claire Leadbetter and her friends at Guildford College, for whom days at college can feel as if she is trapped in a novel by Franz Kafka. Hope it ends better for you all!

Kebabs *noun* internet speed

'My **kebabs** are so slow in the valleys.'

Dino Holmes and his dad in Wales.

Kents *noun* rubbish, tat

'That's **kents**.'

Sue Rogers and family, 'after the name of a local second-hand shop in the eighties and nineties'.

Kiff *adjective* great, wonderful, excited

'I am so **kiff** about going on holiday'

Mrs M Campbell, who says it was originally used by children in the 1940s and '50s.

Kinathy *noun* compassion or empathy for a senior citizen battling against forces such as wind and rain for all he or she is worth

> 'I feel such **kinathy** for poor old Mrs Trellis having to walk all the way to the post office in the rain.'

Valerie Jane Morley and others in her 'sleepy village'.

Kipple *verb* to slice the ball, whilst playing golf

> 'Exceedingly good **kipple**, Tiger!'

Richard Burnell and his regular golf partners at Hallowes Golf Club in Sheffield. 'The word kipple started around twenty-five years ago. I was a prolific slicer of the golf ball and also a lover of Mr Kiplings Almond Slices. The Mr Kipling catchphrase was "Exceedingly good cakes". I changed cakes to slices, thus every time I sliced the golf ball it became a Kipple.'

Kitchroom *noun* a living/dining area adjacent to and visible from the kitchen but not in the same room as the kitchen

> 'And this is our **kitchroom** . . .'

Peter Bailey and his family and friends use this conflation of kitchen and living room. Watch out for Kitchroom Table Lingo!

Kizey *noun* squirrel

> 'The **kizeys** have eaten all the bird food again.'

Venetia Horton invented this when she was a child, and it is now used by the Harrison and Horton families.

MEERA SYAL
Comedienne, actress and writer

Kana for thought

Here are some of my words.

Kana: I use this a lot to mean food. I'm pretty sure it is of Punjabi origin.

Within our family we have talked of **shame-shame** whenever a toddler takes off his or her nappy. My mother used it, and I used it. I think it comes simply from the so-called shame of running around with nothing around your bottom!

Pindoo is a derogatory word to describe somebody who is a country bumpkin or an idiot. I think it is what we call a Hinglish word.

Chaddies are underpants. And it's used in the context of 'kiss my chaddies', which I guess in itself means 'kiss my arse'. I don't know where it comes from.

And **freshie**. I used this when I was a teenager, as did my friends. It stems from people who have just or freshly got off the boat as immigrants to Britain. But we use it towards somebody who is behaving as if they have just got off the boat. In other words, they are naive or a bit backward. Yes, it is a bit rude coming from immigrants from India.

We also use funny words just within our family. For example, my father's younger brother is known as **Cha-cha**. And because we have so many aunties and uncles, one uncle is called **Pink Panther** and another **Overbite**.

Klaw *noun* used to denote a walk when within earshot of a dog

   'Come on Spot, time for your **klaw**!'

Dr Paul Jonathan Fray. 'The word walk backwards; used when not wanting to excite the dog into a frantic lather (the dog having learnt the word "walk").' Paul's family have also coined 'oinob' (bonio) and 'Sel' (Les the gardener). Tnaillirb!

Klemmerise *verb* the process of accidental distortion, revision or addition to the English language

   'There you go, English Project, **klemmerising** again.'

Jonathan Cate and his friends created this while spending a year abroad in Spain. 'I created this term, based upon the surname of one Andreas Klemmer of Berlin, to describe the numerous neologisms he accidently created through his direct translations of German into English, or his combination of terms to create a new word. His English was very good, and it always came as a surprise to him to discover that the words or concepts he created were not, in fact, genuine English terms. Several of the terms created became common parlance among the English-speakers of our extended group in Spain.'

Kraser *adjective* (pronounced krarzer) foul and disgusting

   'Yuck, that's absolutely **kraser**!'

Sarah Helmy: 'My sister had a dream many years ago which featured a voice saying "anagram of kraser cup". She felt that solving the anagram would provide her with the meaning of life and the secrets of the universe. She has never cracked it but it gave us kraser, which she felt meant foul.'

Add your own KTL words here

word _____

definition _____

sample _____

_____

word _____

definition _____

sample _____

_____

word _____

definition _____

sample _____

_____

Kennel Bowl Lingo

As well as words created in the kitchen, many of you submitted words that describe the behaviour of household pets. These fall into two main categories: words that describe the viler activities of cats and dogs and those, often with much affection, which capture the habit of a particular animal.

Boking is Bill Hayhurst's evocative word for the sound that cats or dogs make when being sick (you can almost hear the gagging 'kk' in the poor animal's throat), and skadunk is the name Mandy Dewison gives to dog poo, again imagining the sound of the unfortunate foot squelching its way through the brown stuff.

The verb to **lyric** seems far too nice to describe the action of a cat spraying on foliage. But the keen eyes of Colin Taylor have seen the delicate quivering and trembling of a cat's tail and clearly found it to be worth singing about. While mallawowing seems just right for cats howling at night for Michael Harvey.

Many of you have observed in painstaking detail the actions of your pets. Anthony Glanville gives us *gongle* for dogs gnawing away at large bones. Scooter-bum from Ian Mackenzie clearly evokes the act of a dog rubbing its backside along the carpet or across grass.

Snergle (from Sally French) describes the curious way in which a cat pushes its head against you in an act of affection calculated to get you to rub and scratch its head. **Nudgle** is what cats or dogs do to Andy Wiggins when they prod him to get his attention. While *shnert* (from Julia Ellis) describes the noise a contented dog makes when expelling air through its nostrils to express its happiness after being given a treat!

And having a pet not only stimulates Kitchen Table Lingo, it also calls for linguistic low cunning. Andy Jenner uses **mump** to describe the battle of wills that takes place when a pet, usually a dog, sits alongside you as you eat and gazes longingly at you and your food. Or you can join Paul Fray in resorting to **klaw** because of the advanced literacy skills of his dog, ever in hope that he will be taken for a walk!

L

Ladgin *adjective* embarrassing or uncool (often shortened to **ladge**)

'She looked so **ladgin** reading that book.'

Lucy Beacon, who explains: 'It's a versatile word which can be used in various ways such as "She was ladgin", meaning "She was uncool", or "I felt ladged", meaning "I was embarrassed". It's often used with the word "weeny", meaning "very". It's used by people in the City of York – I've never heard it from people without York connections. I've no idea where it came from – my friends and I still use it to this day and have been using it since our teens, nearly twenty years ago. Possibly it's old Yorkshire, but that would be a guess. It wasn't made up by us, it was just there to use.'

Lah-loo *noun* foolish person

'Only a **lah-loo** would come around here speaking like that.'

Anna Fenton, and spoken by her family and other Irish people she knows.

Lardleys *noun* a collection of small objects of sentimental value including gifts, souvenirs and mementoes, as in 'I'll put that with my lardleys'

'When I go into that nursing home I want to have my **lardleys** with me.'

David Batterham, and used by the Batterham family. It is believed to date back at least to the 1920s.

Legs and dresses *noun* the cooling towers and chimneys at old-style power stations

'I like the look of those **legs and dresses**.'

Chris Rayment, and used within the Forster family. It dates back to the 1960s when, on long car journeys, Chris's sister regularly announced that she could see 'legs and dresses'. The family worked out she was referring to cooling towers and chimneys, and the meaning stuck.

Leuchars Junction Question *noun* a question which is better not asked because you will probably not like the answer

> 'The West Lothian question? Now that would be a **Leuchars Junction Question**.'

Gaye Manwaring, who explains that it comes from, and is used around, Leuchars Junction, a small railway station in Fife in Scotland. The derivation is classically Scots. 'A visitor with heavy luggage wanted to get to the opposite platform and asked the stationmaster if he could walk across the track. The stationmaster said that he had to cross via the footbridge. So the visitor struggled up the steps across the bridge and down the other side. Then, another man walked across the track. Angry and tired the visitor asked why the stationmaster had let the other man cross the track. The station-master replied, "He didn't ask." And neither should you. Just play stupid!

Lill *adjective* gaudy, overly decorative and kitsch

> 'Jill's looking a bit **lill**.'

Claire Murgatroyd, who uses it amongst her family and says that the source is TV. 'Years ago on the BBC programme *Yus My Dear*, Arthur Mullard was married to a woman called Lill, whose house and attire were garish and dreadful. Thus anything that is in the style of Lill can also be described as lill.'

Lintox *noun* fool, buffoon, idiot

> 'We need to get this sorted. Are you the **lintox** – or is it me?'

John Berry, who comments: 'The word was created ten years ago in a moment of frustration by engineers working in Sampson House, London, and has been used ever since.'

Liverpolitan *noun* an upmarket alternative to Liverpudlian

> 'Ringo was a Liverpudlian but John and Paul were a bit more **Liverpolitan**.'

John Jay, who comments that it describes a person, place or thing native to or characteristic of Liverpool. It is used by 'a surprising number of people among the chattering classes on Merseyside. I first became conscious of the word in the late 1950s – and its use was boosted immeasurably in the Merseybeat era of the 1960s and '70s.'

Lock *noun and verb* to complete the work on an edit, after which no more changes will be made

> 'When are we going to **lock** *Kitchen Table Lingo: The Movie*?'

Julie Foster, who comments that it is used by people involved in film and TV editing. She doesn't know the source, but adds: 'With the advent of digital systems, which can retain various edits, the terms "soft lock" and "on the latch" indicate an edit which is almost finished, but still subject to tweaks.'

Loishing *noun* teeming rain; a diet of persistent, non-stop soaking rain

> 'Typical Bank Holiday – non-stop **loishing**.'

Ron Green, who says that his family uses it. 'Being brought up in Wales, there was a lot of very wet weather, and this was a word used by my mother to describe really heavy persistent rain. Her roots were in Devon, so there is a possible West Country origin.'

Lumby *adjective and noun* the feeling of being somewhat tired and/or ill. Alternatively, an object, such as a Christmas tree, when its usefulness has markedly deteriorated

'I always feel **lumby** on Boxing Day.'

Michael Reid and friends, who have 'used it in good humour' for many years.

....

Lun *noun* the reflected light of the sun on the ceiling or wall from the face of a wristwatch

'You can just see the cobwebs with this **lun**.'

Mark Cole and his family in Salisbury; Mark says that it was first coined by a nephew when a young child.

....

Lunged *adjective* the way you feel when you have smoked far too many cigarettes

'I've got to stop. I'm feeling right **lunged**.'

Filipe McManus, who says it is used by at least five of his friends. 'It usually comes with a hangover for smokers,' says Felipe, adding that it's derived from 'lung'. Sounds terminal.

....

Lyric *verb* to spray, as used when cats project on to foliage

'Brumsie has just nipped out to **lyric**.'

Colin Taylor and his friends the Browns, who use it to describe 'the quivering nature of the spraying operation, the trembling of the tail and a job well done.' It is based upon the ownership and observation of cats over many years. Just don't get too close.

Add your own KTL words here

word _____

definition _____

sample _____

_____

word _____

definition _____

sample _____

_____

word _____

definition _____

sample _____

_____

M

Mabbedy *adjective* foolish or silly

'You **mabbedy** eejit!'

Maureen Power: 'My brother, who is autistic, created this word. He uses it to describe someone who has done something foolish or silly. My whole family now uses it.'

Maddled *adjective* irritated, niggled or frustrated when things are not quite as they should be

'I'm so **maddled** by the way I've been treated.'

Andrew Sinclair says that it was invented by his mother and is used by various generations of his family.

Mahusive 1. *adjective* very large, enormous
2. *adjective* not huge, not massive, but somewhere in between

'That was **mahusive**.'

Nicola Taylor and Sam James in a creative amalgamation of massive and huge (meaning huge) and S Masefield in an alternatively creative interpretation.

Mallawowing *adjective* the noise made by howling cats at night

> 'For goodness' sake shut the window so I can't hear that **mallawowing**.'

Michael Harvey.

Managerise *verb* to reduce the quality of a service or commodity in an organisation as a result of a management decision that seeks to pretend otherwise

> 'I was thinking that we might **managerise** Terminal 5.'

Andrew Mackay, after discussions of the effects of overpaid management consultants and their effects on organisations.

Mansturise *verb* as a male, to apply moisturiser to your body

> 'Feel unfulfilled? You need to **mansturise**.'

Mick Stoker: 'I was in the shower applying moisturiser when I thought it would be amusing to do a skit of an advert for the product and in a deep manly advert voice said something along the lines of "No more wussy creams for me, I MANSTURISE". My girlfriend nearly wet herself laughing and since then it has stuck.'

Mathom *noun* a useless gift that is passed from person to person

> 'Give me that **mathom**, my precious.'

Susan Eden: 'We see a lot of these in the Oxfam shop where I work.' Used by people who like JRR Tolkein's *The Lord of the Rings*.

....

May-may *verb* a request to make up after a tiff

> 'Can we **may-may**?'

Jeremy Iles, from 'make-make', which is from 'to make up'.

....

Mellox *noun* a relaxed and garrulous state normally induced by a couple of pints and the warmth of the sun on one's back or the glow of an open fire

> 'One more pint and I'll be in the **mellox** state.'

Mike Brennan, his girlfriend and their close friends. 'The word is a portmanteau, coined in the mists of time in either a sunny beer garden or in front of a roaring pub fire, when the words mellow and bollocks accidentally merged. It now gets used on similar occasions when we're feeling the former and talking the latter.' Or in Kitchen Table Lingo terms, a mixture of bibbly and bollotics?

....

Melly *noun* remote control

> 'Did you say you wanted the **melly**?'

Michael Bell in Ireland: 'First used by our daughter when very young. She has hearing loss, of which we were not aware at the time, and probably derives from telly.'

Melutious *adjective* delicious

> 'Mmmm that tastes **melutious**.'

Gwyn Clark, who tells us that it was coined in 1941 by young Ted Dixon on RAF Kissi, Sierra Leone, and is still in use. Ted 'always referred to a good cup of tea as melutious. It became common currency on the camp. When asked about the word Dixon explained that when young he had read on a tea packet instructions to "add boiling water and blend into one mellifluous whole". His juvenile mispronunciation gave rise to the word.'

Mep *verb* the act of a child making a sound or action to show their frustration

> 'Tom **meps** so much when he's trying to walk, but he's nearly got it!'

Thomas Alexander.

Mezza-mezza *noun* shared half and half

> 'Let's go **mezza-mezza**.'

Peter Bailey, along with the six members of his immediate family and now many of his friends and acquaintances, use this handy word 'of Italian origin and a corruption of *meta-meta* (half and half)'.

Mibbely *adjective* the effect of prolonged immersion in water on fingers

> 'I've been in the pool so long my hands have gone all **mibbely**.'

Sarah Le Gras, and used by the Le Gras and King families. 'Invented by Sarah at the age of about four years when having a bath.'

....

Mim *noun* the remains of the pastry from making small jam tarts squashed together and baked between the tart cases

> 'Mmmm that **mim** tastes yummy.'

Used for years by Richard Fox and family in Stratford and London and, according to Richard, should be 'eaten warm straight from the oven'. Mmmm sounds avlexly!

....

Mindle *verb* to walk

> 'Look at her **mindling** along!'

Rob Eady.

....

Misappear *verb* used to describe a missing item that is not permanently lost

> 'Anyone seen my keys? They've **misappeared**.'

Elaine Broom France, whose eight-year-old son first used it to describe his missing football shorts. (Maybe they were on the floordrobe?)

Molligise *verb* to tickle tummy to produce uncontrollable giggling or laughter

> 'Do that once more and I'll **molligise** you.'

Douglas Brennen, who explains that molligising can also be used as a threat before bedtime or at other times to exert parental authority over small children. Invented by ex-pat English Brennen and his family in Rome and Brussels in the 1970s and '80s.

Monkey-shop *noun* large supermarket shopping session

> 'Who's coming with me to Sainsbury's for the **monkey-shop**?'

Andy Hurd and family, although there is a dispute as to whether this is because carrying bags stretches the arms or is the result of images of ape arms sweeping goods off the shelf into the trolley. Puzzling!

Mootang *verb to* wander around aimlessly on the internet

> 'For goodness' sake stop **mootanging** and come and have your supper.'

Julian Harrold, his girlfriend and their friends coined this as the result of a texting error. Could mootanging be the next Google?

Mouppey *adjective* in a rather fragile and grumpy state, feeling sorry for oneself and wanting others to know it

> 'I just want you all to know that I am feeling EXTREMELY **mouppey**!'

Peter Bailey and family. 'It grew from the concept of moping, but an adjective was needed.'

....

Mump *verb* used to describe the situation where a pet (usually a dog) sits alongside you as you eat and gazes longingly at you and your food in an effort to will you into giving it a sample

> 'That dog's **mumping** again!'

Andy Jenner: 'My parents used this word often to describe our Labrador's behaviour and my wife and children and I have continued to use it. I honestly believed it to be a slang expression but was surprised to be told by my cousin that it was a word made up by our grandfather that appears to be unknown outside our family.'

....

Mutilator *noun* remote control

> 'Quick! Grab the **mutilator** and change the channel.'

Anne-Lise Heinrichs: 'We tend to dive for the remote to mute advertisements and irritating people, often yelling "Aaah! Mutilator!" so the mutilator is the thing that mutes stuff!' Take cover if you're near the Heinrichs household!

....

Myzipe *verb* to cause confusion or misunderstanding

> 'Yet again a tabloid paper **myzipes** us all.'

Joseph Dunn and the Dunn family.

The sound a new word makes

Say 'aah'. The 'buzz' of a bee. A 'crackling' fire. In the ABC of words there are thousands which illustrate that most pleasurable of experiences – onomatopoeia – when sound and sense collide.

Kitchen Table Lingo is full of gloriously noisy words.

We can go **bogwurpling** with Samuel Lesley and hear the squelching of thick Norfolk mud. When our clothes get caught up with each other and at the same time seem rather scrumpled you can reach for **bumphled** to help you out, thanks to Angela Moreland.

Sometimes new words sound like close cousins of other words, giving us strong aural clues as to their meaning:

'I see the English cricket team *conbulljulated* again.'

'What a **drizmal** day.'

'That's a bit of an **embuggerance** and it's making me very *frangled*.'

'Tony, will you stop **testiculating** and admit it: you don't know what you're on about!'

'You're gorgeous! Fancy an **improposition** from me?'

Or part of the word hints at a meaning. So a bobbit is a small child bobbing around. The fuss in **cafustulated** keys us in to the anxiety and the 'tulated' bit suggests some kind of condition. And colourbetical is clearly a new spin on alphabetical.

Exclamations such as '**Hork!**', 'Birkenhead!' and '*Shizzle!*' allow speakers to play with words which are not quite as naughty as those that they sound like!

Often there are echoes of that great onomatoteaser (?) Lewis Carroll and his 'Jabberwocky':

'If you don't go to bed now, I'll send for the nibbygorger.'

'That was a **snickersnack** thing to do.'

Who knows – maybe you can actually hear a new Kitchen Table Lingo word being born!

N

Nang *adjective* shrewd, tight-fisted with money, and maybe combining this with a poor, even destitute, appearance

> 'He's loaded but he wears those old trainers because he's **nang**.'

'Ravi', who says that it is used among British Asians because it is derived from the Punjabi word 'nanga', meaning someone who is naked or very poor; a tramp who has status or possessions.

Nadge *noun* a small item of rubbish, waste food, fluff, etc

> 'When I got back from shopping I found the children had filled the sink up with **nadge**.'

Hilary Derby, who says it is used by three generations of the Derby family and their associated friends. It was coined by Grandfather Derby and then passed on to children and grand?children.

Nesh *noun* someone or something from the 'lower half of the Potteries', which is also known as Neck End

> 'From his accent I thought he was **nesh**.'

John Ronan, who says it is used by people in Burslem, Stoke-on-Trent.

IAN McMILLAN

Poet and broadcaster

On yer grod you brussen!

Slang is the engine room of language. That's what is so great, as it stops any attempts to fossilise language, which is not what you want. Slang is the generator of new language.

But having said that, I do also think that the word 'lingo' is a much better word than 'slang'. Slang is slightly frowned upon. I much prefer 'lingo'. It is much friendlier and warmer. And it rhymes with 'bingo', which is also fun.

Nesh: it means to be frightened of the cold. It is used in Barnsley where I'm from, but I think it is used in other parts of South Yorkshire. Obviously it's a bit insulting to call somebody nesh. (See John Ronan's entry for **nesh** on the previous page, which follows the KTL rules more strictly)

Brussen: this means a person who is arrogant or lippy. It's certainly a word I use quite a bit!

Grod: an old push-bike. I know it's used in Doncaster, but I don't know if it's used more widely in South Yorkshire. I've no idea where it came from.

Quack: a segment of an orange. I know it is used in the village of West Ardsley.

Dit-dit: this is our household name for the TV remote control. No idea why.

Camping magazines: now this is a really odd one we use as a phrase in our house to diffuse an argument. My mother used it first. I think it was used as way of getting us to change the subject. Maybe camping magazines were so boring that we'd forget our row.

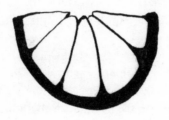

Nibbygorger *noun* an unspecified monster which was used to frighten children into behaving

> 'Up to bed NOW or I'll call in the **Nibbygorger**. He's very hungry . . .'

Letitia Coney of Ashford in Kent, who said that it was probably first used by Lilian Miles, 'aunt extraordinary' in the 1950s and '60s. 'It was truly inspired onomatopoeia, an evocative word for subduing small and naughty children.' Sounds like a cousin-thrice-removed of the Jabberwock.

Nigeling *verb* to cuddle up close

> 'Who did you see **nigeling** at the back of cinemas?'

Rachel Wallace, who explains: 'I started using this word not long after my companion, Nigel, and I met four years ago. As we were always cuddling up together it seemed appropriate to term it after him.' This almost falls into pillow-talk rather than Kitchen Table Lingo but as it's now been taken up by Rachel and Nigel's family members and friends we are delighted to include it.

Noffage *noun* an item that has been thrown away because it has not been used for years, but very shortly afterwards an urgent need is found for it (widely believed to be humanity's single most common experience)

> 'Last week I had three **noffages** – the left-footed wellie, the darts set and that picture of Tony Blair.'

Valerie Bright and her extended family in both the UK and in America. It's believed to have originated in Sawbridgeworth, Hertfordshire, in the early 1970s. (Maybe they threw away the 1960s – and pretty soon regretted it.)

Noggie *noun* the end part of a loaf of bread which is crust on one side

> 'Look, Mum, he's given me the **noggie** again – and he KNOWS I hate the noggie. **Snotfair**.'

Dr Mike Streater, who says it's been used by 'all my family for generations', right back, presumably, to the day when someone had the bright idea of sliced bread.

....

Nonge *noun* the entrance or admission fee

> 'It used to be three bob but now the **nonge** means there's no change out of forty quid.'

John Hardy of Cambridge, who explains that in the early 1990s he took his four-year-old daughter swimming. 'I gave her the money to get in and asked her to be "Guardian of the Dosh". She proudly told her mother that she was "Guardian of the Nonge", and admission fees have been nonge ever since.' (And, you might say, much more expensive as well.)

....

Nooblette *noun* cat (often abbreviated to **noob**)

> 'I hope your **nooblette** isn't going to **lyric**!'

Simon James and his family; Simon comments that it's been in use in the family for as long as he can remember – at least thirty years – and was probably invented by his father.

Noodles *greeting* goodnight

> '**Noodles**, sweet ladies. **Noodles**!'

Polly Powis, her family and their associates, who say it is derived from 'nighty-noodles'.

Noofle *verb* to lick the corner of a handkerchief and vigorously wipe around the mouth and chin of a small child

> 'After that ice cream I had to **noofle** her for about five minutes.'

Alec Hamilton and his family, who used it originally in Gloucestershire. It has now spread further afield through use by Alec's grown-up children who recall the experience. 'It's completely made up,' says Alec, 'but perhaps echoing the objecting "noof" sound made by children to whom it is done.'

Norm *noun* remote control

> 'Just why exactly did you take **norm** into the shower?'

Michelle Hanks, who says it is derived from 'auto-norman' (although she has no idea what, when or who auto-norman was).

The story behind **normie**

normie *noun*; a person without a disability

Language unites but it can also divide. It can be a way of separating 'us' from 'them' in ways which can be rude and offensive. For Mark Dunn it has become a matter of resentment that there is a whole battalion of words that classify – and maybe put down – people with disabilities, while nothing equivalent could be applied to those who were able-bodied.

That is why he was pleased to contribute **normie** to Kitchen Table Lingo. As someone with hypermobility syndrome (an extreme form of double-jointedness which prematurely wears away the joints) Mark has experienced the loss of his ability to walk – and along with that his job – in a unique way. Although he is now part of what might be called a disabled community he is militant about the insensitive way that he feels society at large, and the government in particular, neglects the individuality of disabled people.

He is not alone. On websites such as BBC's 'Ouch' forum there is a growing movement to redefine the terms in both directions. That was where **normie** came from, as a first step towards righting the balance. 'There are a multitude of names used for disability but none for able-bodied people,' says Mark.

'Even the term "able-bodied" is only used when talking about disability. **Normies** have a need to box things and apply labels to anything that differs from their perception of normal. In these days of supposed equality it is only fair we should have the right to apply a label to people without disabilities.'

Odd man out?

Through the medium of the internet Mark and others are also intent on finding new words for people with disabilities. **Odd** is Mark's suggestion, but also under consideration are words such as **discom** and **disabilispher**. There is also a move to bring back 'cripples' (in the same way that the gay community embraced the word 'queer' and thus rid it of its power to hurt). As to other 'private' language, Mark is particularly keen on **fripples** to address the issue of 'fake cripples'. 'The whole political correct-ness approach towards language is a disaster,' he says. 'Let people say what they like and I'll tell them when I find it offensive.' And, presumably, if **normies** find Mark offensive they can tell him that too.

Northsouthers *noun* trousers with wide legs that remain in place while still allowing you to walk briskly

> 'It's ridiculous – in the dark I put on my **northsouthers** inside out.'

Angela Griffiths, who says occupational therapists at Charing Cross Hospital invented it in the 1980s to describe their NHS uniform trousers.

See also **eastwesters**

Nosling *adjective* cute or sweet (especially when applied to a cat)

> 'If only you could look as **nosling** as Tigger.'

Helen Ferguson, who attributes it to her siblings' description of her cat's appearance with ears flattened so her face became sleeker and pointier. It is derived from 'nosling gosling' (in other words 'cute like a gosling' – and that is pretty cute, isn't it?).

Noynoy *noun* a small piece of cloth used as a comforter

> 'Oops – I think we left Jenny's **noynoy** on the plane!'

Jenny Hawkins and her extended family of about ten people. Derived from an adaptation of 'nite-nite'. Currently applied to any object that gives comfort.

Nu-nu *noun* a baby's dummy or pacifier

> 'Isn't forty a bit old for sucking that **nu-nu**?'

Edward Beedham and his family. Inspired by the sound made when sucking it.

Nubby *noun* computer memory stick

> 'Edward's gone and lost the **nubby** with all the KTL on.'

'Jeanie' and her family. 'It just seemed to evolve as a word to describe the tiny object.'

Nudgle *verb* prodding by an animal (usually a dog or a cat) when it wants attention, and the effect of shifting a human arm until it's petted

> 'Did you see the way Sinbad **nudgled** up to Simon?'

Andy Wiggins and family. 'We derived it from the verb "nudge". Initially we said the dog was "nudging" which quickly became "nudgling". This sounded a warmer and more friendly word which described better what the dog was doing and the attention it required.'

Nungy *noun* milk (and breast milk)

> 'There's no **nungy** for my cereal. Simon gave it all to Sinbad.'

Andrew Shone and his immediate family. 'The word was invented by our eldest child when a toddler. It was then adopted by the second child and is still in use ten years later.'

O

Obgollick *adjective* awkward; out of sorts

'You seem a bit **obgollick** today.'

Anne Priest.

Obsoque *noun* marmite on toast

'**Obsoque** 4 t?'

Julian Harrold: 'A predictive text error which stuck because it was shorter.'

Oggsnitch *noun* a nerd who informs on someone, or tells tales, to the authorities

'Watch out, the **oggsnitches** are coming.'

Peter Shepherd and schoolchildren across Hertfordshire, Essex and Middlesex in the 1960s. 'A group of nerds at Cheshunt Grammar School in Herts were studying an old Celtic alphabet called Ogam. Being kids, they also used these symbols to convey comments about those outside their group. However, in-fighting within the group led to some members snitching, or grassing, on others, by informing the outsiders what derogatory things had been written about them by insiders. These folk who gave away the secrets were referred to as oggsnitches, and the word spread through schools in the area and became used as a general term for a nerd who told tales, especially to teachers, or the authorities in general.' Very Harry Potter!

Oinky *adjective* affected with car sickness, nauseated by car travel

'Mum, can you stop the car – I'm feeling really **oinky**.'

Matthew Stevens: 'When asked by mother to describe more accurately how I was feeling after complaining of feeling sick whilst in the back of the car I replied that I felt oinky.'

....

Oldtama *noun* an old, famous, handsome man

'Isn't Edward Fox an **oldtama**?'

Richmon Bash Garbah in Ghana.

....

Oofah doofa *noun* remote control

'**Oofah doofa**, please.'

Neil Sleeman-Smith, Hazel Reed, David Tweedale, Claire Friend and Emma Wood all use this, some attributing it to Noel Edmonds in the 1980s.

....

Oom-phoo *adjective* feeling unwell, off-colour

'Are you OK? You look a bit **oom-phoo**.'

Fernando José Cruz in Spain from the Inca language Quechua meaning just that.

Ostrich *verb* to stall and refuse to open brown envelopes, particularly when you suspect bills – or letters from school, etc

'I'm **ostriching** that one – it looks like the gas bill.'

Caroline Miles and her friends when they want to put their head in the financial sand.

Add your own KTL word here

word   _____

definition   _____

sample   _____

_____

P

Papwack *noun* a small blob of something that is slimy or sticky and probably of organic origin

> 'Ee-hh! Wayne touched the **papwack** – then he licked it!'

Lorraine van Dam, who adds that it is normally best 'not to investigate too closely'. The word can also apply to 'sticky glue on items from which the label has been removed'. Her mother and members of the family use it. 'Who knows the derivation?' she says. 'But it is a very useful word in the domestic context.' We reluctantly agree.

Patsches *noun* slippers, house shoes

> 'You wore your **patsches** to school! What did the teacher say?'

Elsa Hamaz, who says it is used within her family and provides the explanation, 'Potschen is a South Tyrolean dialect word for house shoes. I come from this area and I speak this German/Austrian dialect with my children who grew up in the UK. My husband does not speak German, but has always spoken English to our children apart from the word "patsches" for slippers. The German word was anglicised by adding "es" for the plural, instead of "en" as for the German plural.' All good for Anglo-German relations, then.

Patty *noun* a ball that is poorly hit (for example, with the wrong part of the racket or wrong angle) so that it bounces off the racket feebly

'Murray hit a **patty** in Beijing.'

Helen Ferguson, who says that she and her siblings used it as a result of 'playing tennis in the garden with rubbish plastic rackets'. The derivation is mostly from the verb 'to pat' but also has subtle hints of adjective to imply flat (as in 'cow pat').

Peglomania *noun* a compulsive obsession to collect clothes pegs

'He tried to patent a new drug for **peglomania** but he was hung out to dry.'

Michael Bradley, whose girlfriend invented it in reponse to his proclivities in this direction. It is now in common use, apparently, amongst other peg collectors (plus their wives, girlfriends and sundry supporters) throughout Gloucestershire and Cheshire. Washing lines beware.

Peng *adjective* attractive physically

'Do women think Lawrence is **peng**?'

Michael Clarke and people from Nottingham, but also Daisy from North London and Heather Dooley and her mates.

The story behind paragateaux

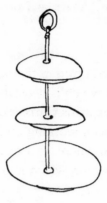

paragateaux *noun*; a cake stand, often three-tiered, of the kind used to serve afternoon tea. From Old French *paré de gâteaux* – adorned with cakes

Universities might seem to be talking shops but what happens when they run out of words? What do they do when they come across critical gaps in the English language, well endowed though it is, for vital aspects of life in the early twenty-first century such as, for example, a multi-layered cake stand?

That was the challenge facing Oxford-educated physicist Chris Simpson and his colleagues at York University when confronted by a linguistic deficit in Betty's Tea Shop. Even the waitress, apparently, was left speechless. With **paragateaux** they cracked it. But even Chris admits that it is a mite unusual to orchestrate so many great minds to meet such a basic naming need. Hence the inauguration of what might be called the groundbreaking 'York School' of Kitchen Table Lingo consisting of Chris Simpson, Eilis Mullally, Rob Kettell, Ruth Curtice, Louise Eggett, Matthew Wright, Gayle Johnson, Nikki Allford, Richard Sharp and other friends.

A word telescope

'There's a whole subculture in the office and amongst my own uni friends which is dedicated to finding words for new concepts,' explains Chris. 'For example, one of the projects we've been working on for years is a word for the phenomenon where, as a result of laziness one adopts a course of action which is actually going to make a job harder in the long run because you can't be bothered to put in a little bit of extra effort at the start.'

In Chris's case he has a long-standing addiction to word invention going back to his school days. One of his first endeavours was the verb to **fussell**, which means to create fuss and hassle out of a situation. However, his word that is truly at the cutting edge of technology is **synokia**, roughly equivalent to synonym, except that it draws on texting, so that the first text word typed in means the same as the intended word. Hence 'book' means 'cool'. 'This system is coming into use quite a lot, but there is no word we knew to describe it.'

Well, the answer has now been found courtesy of Kitchen Table Lingo. **Synokia**: you read it here first.

Peshawar *noun* the powder that falls from a Peshawari naan bread as you break it

> 'That naan was covered in **peshawar**.'

Bill Isham and his family; Bill points out that large amounts of peshawar usually indicate good-quality naan bread. The word fills a gap in the language like a naan fills a hole in the tummy.

Pfot *verb* to open a new jar of, for example, coffee

> 'Can you **pfot** that, please, Mr Barista?'

KT van Santen and family; it is inspired by the sound of the teaspoon piercing the seal.

Phaser *noun* remote control

> 'Let's use the **phaser** to boldly go where no human intelligence has previously penetrated. How about Channel 5?'

'Rosa' in Scotland, who comments, 'My parents started it years ago after watching an episode of *Star Trek*.'

Photocopier syndrome *noun* the state of hysteria caused by an inability to operate an electronic or technical device.

> 'Excellent news! Treatment for **Photocopier syndrome** is now available on the NHS.'

Martin Chambers who explains, mysteriously, that it has been used by his family following an 'incident in a newsagent's'. 'This state is normally marked by incoherent and inappropriate attempts to communicate with and/or express hostility to inanimate objects,' says Martin. It is widely believed to be the UK's second-fastest-growing mental health problem after **peglomania**.

Pickin *verb* starting to rain

> 'Put the picnic away it's **pickin**.'

A Hanford from South Wales, who believes it originates from a Welsh translation.

Pilot *noun* remote control

> 'Who's kidnapped the **pilot**?'

'Bobby' (from Scotland), his Polish girlfriend and Australian flatmate. 'My Polish girlfriend, an academic, introduced the word to us. It seems to make sense – given pilot is also a word for guide, navigator, direction-finder, etc.'

Pinger *noun* remote control

> 'You're not listening to me. Pass the **pinger**.'

David Nicoll, who uses it with his family and explains, 'I think I may have introduced this as I work in IT, where "ping" is a well-known term for communicating with something.' Also Kay Sumpner and the Travers family.

Pingly *adjective* feeling unwell, 'off-colour', headachy

> 'I don't think Amy should go down the pub. She's feeling **pingly**.'

L. Millar and family.

Pisspotical *adjective* stupid, with reference to an idea/thought/suggestion

> 'Abolish 10p tax? That's **pisspotical**.'

Bryan Walker and people in North Yorkshire. 'I first heard it when my father was in hospital in Northallerton and it was used by an old farmer in the next bed to him.' Also Paul Whitfield.

Pizzeltwisted *adjective* feeling extremely cold

> 'Football in February is guaranteed to make you **pizzeltwisted**.'

Arthur S J Miles, and used in the Connelly family. Its origins lie in pizzel (a need to urinate) and twisted (crossing one's legs) and relates to the effect of cold on the bladder.

Pleasement *noun* liking

> 'I prefer holidaying by myself. You can do things to your **pleasement**.'

Garry Coffey and family and friends; Garry explains that the word 'originated from my mum's side of the family, and has been used ever since'.

Plinker *noun* remote control

> 'Right, which of you plonkers has the **plinker**?'

Lloyd Shove, Alan Paterson and R Love from Hampshire.

Ploggo *adjective* very full after eating; stuffed

> 'How can you put any more away? I'm **ploggo**.'

Paul Readman and his family, who think their grandparents invented it.

Plonker *noun* remote control

> 'Here's the man with a plan for the **plonker**.'

The whole Wilkinson family, including the extended family in Ireland and the USA and Canada. 'We have always called it the plonker. No one knows why. Perhaps because that is what it does – it plonks!

SIR TREVOR McDONALD

Journalist and *News at Ten* anchor

Don't give me picong; just tell it straight!

Here are some of my Kitchen Table Lingo words.

Picong: we used it in Trinidad and I still do. I would use it in the context of 'somebody giving me picong'. It means that this person is not really telling the truth – that what he or she says should be taken with a pinch of salt. I have no idea where it came from except that in Trinidad a lot of words came from French, Dutch and Spanish because they at various times occupied the island or at the very least had very strong trade links. Maybe it was like the French word, *piquant*?

Commess: my mother would use it to mean a state of total confusion. I like it – it's like a complete mess, which is where it may have come from.

Bachanal: we would say 'what a bachanal' to mean what a cock-up. Again, it's a word I would still use but I have no idea if others in England who came from the West Indies still use it. Obviously it must have come from 'bacchanalia' – a sort of drunken orgy.

I used to be a real stickler for language, but I have changed my thinking more recently. I think this is because I have realised more and more that the English language has this constantly changing nature, which we should accept. It is frankly the marvel of the English language. However, I am still a stickler for grammar. I think correct grammar enriches language.

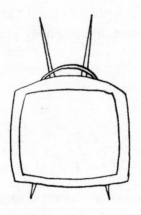

Plotch *verb* to eat noisily

> 'I was sitting near Stephen in the Ivy but couldn't over-hear what he was saying because my companion **plotches**.'

Patricia Thomas, whose father invented it because he did not like sitting with people who had noisy eating habits.

Podger *noun* remote control

> 'You're podgy because your only exercise comes from that **podger**.'

Colin Usher and family.

Pogged *adjective* to be absolutely full after eating

> 'I'm so **pogged** I could peg out.'

Alastair Stewart, Charles Denison and family in Australia and England who say it originally came from Yorkshire (but spell it just 'poged'), John Wilkins and family, Lin Bridges (who comments that it is 'just another word that my little brother used one day aged eight, that stuck') and Bill Hollowell (who says: 'This was coined several years ago by elder daughter Lynn after a memorable Christmas lunch. It has been used ever since').

The story behind **poddle**

Poddle *verb* the action of a cat kneading on a soft blanket

One of the extraordinary features of Kitchen Table Lingo is the number of times that an individual (or individual family) invents a word and then we find that exactly the same term has been coined, entirely independently, by someone else.

A good example of this is **poddle**, which describes the actions of a cat as it kneads the soft surface on which it is lying. Both Gill Cavanagh and the Thewlis family lay claim to this and each has a very clear and unique memory of when it was invented.

In Gill Cavanagh's case the word just burst spontaneously into her awareness without any thought. The cat concerned was a certain Cleo (sadly now departed) who meant an enormous amount to Gill. Studying the movement of the cat but without having a word to describe it clearly bothered her – and her subconscious got to work.

'The starting point may have been "pommelled", but that clearly was not what Cleo was doing so I needed something else. Without thinking about it, the word poddled popped into my head, and I immediately started to use it. But it is the only word I've ever invented.'

Capturing the action

Interestingly enough, however, Gill has had a lifelong interest in words and, as a child, constantly read the dictionary following a trail of words from one page to the next. 'It was not just a work of reference, it was a treasure chest of discovery.'

In the case of the Thewlis version it was a 'very contented Burmese' who triggered the invention and, perhaps, it was the condition of contentment that sparked the wish to name and thereby take possession of it – rather like Adam in the Garden of Eden. As it happens, lots of Kitchen Table Lingo relates to cats so when the psycho-linguists start following this up they might like to work out the emotional drive behind cat-speak.

Pokery *noun* remote control

> 'Please don't juggle with the jiggery **pokery**.'

Sian Evans, who comments, 'On having a remote control years ago I continually forgot its name and resorted to "the jiggery pokery". That seems to be most people's reason for customising the remote!

Pollywocket *noun* the plastic wallet for protecting individual sheets of paper

> 'I'll barter you twelve **pollywockets** for twenty elastic bands and rubber.'

Mike Sexton and employees of Home Leasing. 'People in the office are always asking for one of these plastic wallets,' says Mike. 'I believe that Diane Clark first used this term ten years ago as a slip of the tongue. Now all of our employees use it.'

Ponk *verb* to use the car horn, i.e., 'Ponk the horn'

> '**Ponk** the horn, Lewis, and they'll soon get out of the way.'

Iain Harris, whose eldest son misheard 'Honk' as a small child as 'Ponk' but this seems so descriptive it has stuck so far for more than twelve years

Ponker *noun* a term of endearment which has multi-applications including, in particular, to cats, small children and partners

> 'Hello, little **ponker**. What have you been up to?'

Lizzie Kingston, who says it's been used in her family for at least forty years.

Poob *noun* an unsavoury or malodorous person

> 'I was sitting next to a **poob** all the way from Newcastle.'

The Furlong family.

....

Pook *noun* the round part of a jigsaw piece that fits into the 'hole' of the adjoining piece

> 'All I've got left are two pieces with missing **pooks**.'

Marie Thomas, who has used it with family and friends since she was young. 'As a child, when trying to identify the pieces I gave it that name. For example, "Can you see a piece with a blue pook to fit here?" or "Can you see a three-pook?" and so on.'

....

Poppy *adjective* describes the way in which the skin looks on the hands when they have been in the water a long time

> 'Hands that do dishes always come out **poppy**.'

Fay Andrews and her family, who explain that it was coined by Fay's mum 'needing to find a word to describe how hands look so as to get young children out of the bath (probably about forty years ago)'.

See also **mibbely**

....

Porkulant *adjective* a bit overweight

> 'I love those celeb mags which show stars looking **porkulant**.'

Pete Bates, family and friends; Pete attributes the word to 'fat as a pig, that is a porker'.

Potiater *noun* remote control

'Giles has dropped the **potiater** in the potty again.'

Alan Drew, who says it was first used by his three-year-old son Simon in 1976 and has been applied by the family ever since.

Potterati *noun* everything relating to Harry Potter

'I hear there's been a fresh outbreak of **potterati** on Ealing Broadway.'

Katherine Anderson and her family. It was coined by her husband to deal with all the media hype surrounding the arrival of each book and film. Perhaps, now, the phenomenon may be on the wane.

Add your own KTL word here

word

definition

sample

SUSIE DENT

TV personality

You're **potatoes**

Susie Dent, the resident word expert on Channel 4 TV's *Countdown*, explains that many of her family words derive from Dr Johnson's Dictionary. 'There's **pundle**, a pithy word which Johnson defines as 'a short, fat woman', and **mullgrubs**: a tummy ache. They are still so vivid even after 250-odd years.'

When it comes to Kitchen Table Lingo, however, the word that stands out is **potatoes**, which is Susie's husband and daughter's way of telling people – primarily Susie – to stop daydreaming.

'The story behind it is a *Test the Nation* TV quiz on language a few years back, on which I was a judge,' explains Susie. 'It was live, and scary, and I was so relieved to get through Part One unscathed that, after the break, I started to enjoy myself. And my mind drifted, until I heard Anne Robinson ask 'So, what's the rule here Susie?' All I could remember is that the last quiz question had included the word **potatoes** – it was a spelling question – and so that word, followed by a nervous question mark, was my not-so-clever response.

'Happily I was shown mercy, but now have to live with a lifetime's teasing from my family.'

Q

Queedle *verb* to lean or rock back on a chair so that only the back two legs are on the floor

> 'Stop **queedling** or you'll hurt yourself.'

Andy P and Kathy Brady submitted this independently. Andy tells us: 'I learnt this word from an ex-girlfriend's family and have found it very useful particularly as I am now a primary school teacher! It is almost always used in the classroom in the context of, "Shaun/Stuart/Charlie, etc, stop queedling," and Kathy remembers it being used in her childhood.

Quincy *noun* a debate or debrief after an event

> 'There goes Dad doing a **quincy** again on last night's match.'

Liam Kearns, from the 1970s TV show of the same name.

Quinkiedink *noun* a coincidence

> 'What a wonderful **quinkiedink** to see you here!'

Valerie Branston.

Add your own KTL words here

word

definition

sample

word

definition

sample

word

definition

sample

Language defecit

There will always be big global words like **Google** spread by the Web. Or words which emerge from specific commercial transactions which we all make, such as **PIN number**. And others which arrive with a hint of humour when celebrity and human activity meet, like the **Wag**.

But we want to savour the thrill of more domestic linguistic pleasures. For at the heart of Kitchen Table Lingo is a strong conviction that very many English words start or are given life in our homes. That's why we at The English Project want to be in at the birth of words and marvel as they travel around families and friends.

An enduring challenge which has led to the creation of many Kitchen Table Lingo words is when, quite simply, the language is not up to the job. There's a thought or an idea but not yet a good word for it. Or more commonly, as in the case of the remote control (see pages 12–13), we have words but they are either too unmemorable or too numerous. And that's when the power of Kitchen Table Lingo kicks in. What, for example, do you call 'a large filling breakfast'? 'What's the word for 'severe diarrhoea' in polite society?

And how exactly do you capture in a single word 'that relaxed and garrulous state, normally induced by a couple of pints and the glow of an open fire'? Search Kitchen Table Lingo to find out!

New namings

Your mail-order box of goodies spills out a shower of white polystyrene bits which then litter your floor. Why, they must be **croffles**!

You tell a joke which leaves an awkwardness in the room. It's a *bear-farm*.

The heap of clothes, replete with a strange teenage logic, is in fact a **floordrobe**.

You ask someone going abroad to 'do you a favour and purchase you a specific item'. One (odd) word, *gnome*, replaces ten in an instant! It may not last, but it's a glorious attempt!

You receive a card telling you that you can now book your hospital appointment online at a time to suit you. Elated and amazed, you log on. No appointment slots in the next weeks are available and the system refers you to a telephone number. You call and are connected to a barely audible answer machine that you suspect is rarely listened to. Someone is clearly trying to improve your experience as a patient, but it takes just one word to sum up the reality of all of this for you – **managerise**. You have been **managerised**, misled for a moment into thinking that service might improve but you are really the victim of poor management.

Our favourites

Some words have particularly appealed to us.

Ever thrown away something, possibly even taken it to a car boot sale or flogged it on eBay only to rue your decision because moments later you realise that you need the very item urgently and with a new-found desperation? It's a *noffage*.

Or perhaps you have been on a foreign holiday, enjoyed a beautiful orange liqueur under a moonlit sky with a new best friend and, on your final day, purchased a bottle to take home. Unpacking your case a few days later in the cold light of a British sky you realise that you have made a terrible mistake. What seemed delicious and stylish is gauche and ridiculous now that you are back home. It is, of course, a **dacey**.

Many of the Kitchen Table Lingo words in this book will never make it into the *OED*. But, if they hit the spot, some certainly will. A significant number will give their users untold pleasures along the way. And every single word is an actor in the unfolding stories of the English Language. Happy **klemmerising**!

Which words have tickled your fancy? Tell us now by going to www.englishproject.org/KTL

R

Radge *noun* a bad mood, ill-humour

> 'Gordon's in a **radge** because no one wants to be in his gang any more.'

Magda Bannister, who uses it with her two siblings and mother. 'No idea where it came from, but it was used by my younger brother as a ten-year-old, and it has become family lingo ever since.'

Rail *noun* a mixture of hailstones and rain

> 'One ball bowled and the **rail** came down.'

Cathy.

Raj *particle* affirmative

> 'Regime change? **Raj**.'

Scott McDonald, who uses it with his friends as a short version of 'roger' as in 'roger that' which means 'yes'. (We guess.)

Ram *adjective* disgusting, unappealing

> 'I know it's **ram** but the alternative is school dinners.'

Justine MacArthur and citizens of Bridlington, East Yorkshire. 'It's been in use in Bridlington since I was a child, and my friends' children use it regularly,' says Justine. 'No one I know outside of Bridlington uses it or has heard of it being used in this way.'

Rarrel *noun* a code word used to avoid comment in front of a third party

> 'So who's being made redundant?'
>
> '**Rarrel**.'

Farman Kaveh and friends such as Salman Saffary and others. 'My friends and I often found we were in a position where we had a story to tell or something to say to someone but diplomatically could not do so due to parents/partners/others being able to hear,' explains Farman. 'I created this word to get around this problem so that we'd each be aware we had something to say. Often just saying the word implies the answer you want to give. For example, the question, "What ended up happening between you and that girl last night?" could be as good as answered with a simple "Rarrel". We've been using it for fifteen-odd years now. Clearly it's a word that would be a nice discovery but could never truly fall into widespread use because that would defeat the point.' Ah well, the cat's out of the bag now.

Rarve *verb* to flail around, to push and pull

> 'Don't **rarve** me around!'

Kate Richardson and her mum, sister and nana. 'It has always been in the family,' says Kate, who adds that her nana is ninety.

Rasbas *noun* the browned skin found on a rice pudding after it has been baked in an oven

'It's my turn for the **rasbas**!'

Brian Scallon and his family. Brian comments: 'Sweet rice pudding made with milk and sugar and baked in the oven is not as popular as it was when I was a child. I would compete with my siblings for the chance to have the rasbas on my portion.'

....

Rass *adverb* way of negating the previous statement. Equivalent to 'not'

'House prices have increased this year – **Rass**.'

Charlotte Foster and the Class of 2008 at Wymondham College. 'It was randomly used by Ashley Seager and caught on with the rest of the student population,' says Charlotte.

....

Rastcrost *adjective* harrassed, confused, annoyed

'Just reading this makes me so **rastcrost**.'

Anthea Hall and family members. 'It's been used by my mother and family since the 1930s or '40s.'

....

Rat pile *noun* a growing collection, particularly of papers, that demands attention but is not getting it

'Edward, please explain why your office is full of **rat pile**?'

David Squire, who says family members use it, but he first heard it from his wife. Strangely enough we know the feeling.

Raticaha *noun* bath rack

> 'Put the ducks next to the ships in the **raticaha**.'

Libby Davis, who explains that it was used by her great-grandparents and everyone else in the family ever since. 'It's always been used in the family,' says Libby. 'Great-grandfather thought everyone used this word and went into an ironmonger's and asked for one!' The shop assistant is still searching, we understand.

Raunj *verb* to fidget about restlessly, especially when sitting or lying on chair/sofa or when in bed

> 'Harriet, do stop **raunjing**. It's distracting everyone else.'

Marjorie Cavanagh and her mother and family. 'It was used throughout my childhood in Gorton, Manchester.'

Redskins *noun* the workers who applied the red lead to ships and submarines in the Barrow shipyard.

> 'What time do the **redskins** knock off?'

Dave Doughty, who explains it was used by shipyard workers. 'Although red lead was last used in the 1980s the men still retained the name,' says Dave. 'Unfortunately the department no longer exists. There are only a small number of redleaders left within the yard – a truly dying breed. They were also known as reds or skins. Due to the awkward nature of the work they were often covered in the paint they used. Hence the word.'

Rees-Mogg *noun* remote control

> 'Rees-Mogg isn't working.'

Sue Campbell, who says her family used it because Lord Rees-Mogg was regarded as 'controlling television from a distance'.

Remy *noun* remote control

> 'You can't have the **remy** until after *Big Brother*.'

Sinead Cregan and family.

Resurrectomy *noun* vasectomy reversal

> 'Now you've had your **resurrectomy** I suppose that we'll need that loft extension.'

Sofia Ames, who comments that the term was coined by her brother when her husband had his vasectomy reversal in 2000. Quite a start to the new millennium.

Ribble *verb* to rub a ribbon or label between your fingers as a comforter

> 'I can only sleep when I **ribble**.'

Jan Knibbs, who explains that her daughter, Alice, used the word to describe what she was doing to a ribbon or label whilst sucking her thumb.

Ripon *noun* a bargain

> 'If you've got the money there are plenty of **ripons** out there. But only the rip-off merchants can afford them.'

Jenny Saville, her family and friends. 'We made this up many years ago to be the opposite of a rip-off.'

Rit *noun* a small pimple-like mole but barely attached to the skin

> 'Do you think the clinic could deal with my **rits**?'

Jacqueline Tricker and used by her mum and family. 'We're not sure where it comes from, but it could be Suffolk dialect.'

Ritsy *noun* rabbit

> 'Lettuce with oil and mayonnaise? Luxury for the **ritsy**.'

Max Hardwicke and used by family and friends. It's derived from baby talk (but not baby rabbits').

Rous *adjective* disastrous

> 'Those SATS this year were **rous**.'

James Seago with his whole family and 'everyone at school'. Although coined initially as an abbreviated version of disastrous, its use has now been extended to apply to anything or anyone who is shambolic. According to James, he came up with it with a friend when they were constantly saying 'disaster'. Presumably because they are English cricket fans.

Rumpetty fork *noun* a cake fork

'A **rumpetty fork** please for Mrs Owl on Table 3.'

Glynis Kozma and her family, who explain it's a cousin of the runcible spoon. (A set of rumpetty forks now comes as a matter of course with every **paragateaux**.)

Run-nun *noun* the groove between nose and top lip (technically, the philtrum)

'After the broken nose we had to re-engineer his **run-nun**.'

H V Sherborne and the Stephenson family.

Add your own KTL word here

word   _____

definition _____

sample   _____

_____

The story behind **dacey** and **ruxing**

Dacey *adjective* the assorted clothes and accessories which are bought on holiday, usually abroad, which look ridiculous when you get them home

Ruxing *adjective* touching and embarrassing at the same time

Alys Blakeway contributed two of the first words – **dacey** and **ruxing** – to the Kitchen Table Lingo collection, and that gave her good credentials to take responsibility (along with Madelaine Smith and Sam Byford) for checking and vetting the thousands of others received by The English Project.

'Both words came from my mother's side of the family, which went in for a lot of wordplay and invention. The explanation was that my grandmother was half Irish and had therefore inherited a great enjoyment of the language. That said, **dacey** has a strong Indian connection so, as ever with English, there are a number of different influences at work.'

The checking process to ensure that contributed words meet the Kitchen Table Lingo test is thorough, but Alys has been surprised by how many of the entries have got through.

'It shows that this collection is meeting a need for people who take pleasure in and share their private language,' she says. She has also been impressed by the perseverance of some words, often very localised, through the generations despite the impact of the mass media.

She is now looking forward to another influx of words for Kitchen Table Lingo 2009.

S

Sapperating *adjective* energy-sapping, as occurs in high humidity

> 'This weather's really **sapperating**.'

Geoff Allen.

Schifoid *adjective* tolerably disgusting

> 'Yuk. That's **schifoid**!'

Lydia Vitamaria Wharf-Moltedo, a small group of friends in London and a smaller group in Leeds, a 'compound of *schifo* (Italian for informal) and -oid'

Schneb *noun* nose

> 'I have a runny **schneb**.'

Alex Williams and her family in Wales, most often used in the context of having a cold. 'A nice word my husband picked up from a friend and we have used ever since with our small children.'

Scoff *noun* a scruffy old cloth

> 'Pass me that **scoff**, please.'

Julie Collett, whose family in Yorkshire have used this since the 1950s. 'My mother, almost eighty, thought it may have been in use pre-1950 in the rag trade in Bradford, Yorkshire as a contraction of scruffy old cloth.'

Scoob *noun* a person of higher intellectual capacity. Similar to 'geek' or 'nerd'

> 'Och Bruce, you're such a **scoob**!'

Rachel Hiorns and students at Nairn Academy. Rachel first heard it taking on a teaching post in a Highland school. Also submitted by Laura McKinney and Emma Ritson and as **scoobie** by Jordan Snitch.

Scooter-bum *noun* a dog rubbing his backside along the carpet or across the grass. A descriptive term that fits the action – well known to dog owners

> 'There goes the **scooter-bum**.'

Ian Mackenzie. 'We believe that we invented this word. Our children used to call out the word when the dog was behaving in this unpleasant way so that he could be driven out into the garden.'

Scrage *verb* to scratch or graze yourself

> 'You've **scraged** your knee.'

Sarah Murray, influenced by scratch and graze.

Scrampfer-dampfer *verb* to mix up spaghetti with butter or sauce on the plate using a spoon and fork

> 'Pass me the spoon and fork so I can start to **scrampfer-dampfer**.'

Rachel Godfrey: 'Created by youngest son when asking for help to mix his butter into his spaghetti.'

Scratcher 1. *noun* bed 2. *noun* often used to refer to someone being on the dole, e.g. on the **scratcher**, collecting the **scratcher**

> 'Time for **scratcher**'

Used in New Zealand and contributed by Helen Renwick and also submitted with its second meaning by Neville Walsh in Ireland: 'I think it derives from the fact that someone stays in bed all day if they are on the dole and scratcher has been known to describe the bed.'

Scratty *adjective* being very lucky, as in 'you **scratty** git'

> 'That was a **scratty** goal'

Jonathan Moses.

Screeper *noun* car windscreen wiper

> 'You can turn the **screepers** off now.'

Jeremy Howard: 'While driving, my then four-year-old daughter advised me that as it was raining I should turn on the screepers. It seemed an excellent and shorter name so it stuck.'

Scritch 1. *noun* a comfort blanket 2. *verb* the act of using a comfort blanket

> 'Just give him his **scritch** and he'll stop crying.'

John and Muff Wiltshire and their family.

Scronkle *verb* to move in a furtive manner, rather like scuttling but with a guilty air (especially applied to cats)

> 'You're **scronkling**; what are you up to?'

Tony Wickham: 'My wife needed a word that described the movement of our pet cats – scronkling seemed to describe it best.'

Scrousy *adjective* grubby, decrepit or slightly unpleasant

> 'The house looks really **scrousy** and needs to be cleaned.'

The Duncan/Clarke family. Emma Duncan: 'Originates from one of our cats, Thomas, whose nickname was "Scrousie". He was grubby, decrepit and slightly unpleasant! We use it as an adjective.'

Scruddle *noun* a method of pleasing a cat (and its owner!), halfway between a stroke and a cuddle

> 'I need a **scruddle**!'

Josephine Winwood: 'My husband came up with it whilst stroking our fat cat, who likes her chest being scratched with one hand, whilst we have our other arm around her in a type of cuddle. Has been passed on to family and friends.'

Scrudgings *plural noun* the burnt-on remains of delicious, home-cooked dishes that can be scraped off and fought over after the dish has been served; the tastiest scrapings

'Mmmm, pass me the **scrudgings** please!'

Bryony Richardson in the north east. Definitely Kitchen Table!

....

Scrungle *adjective* in a bad mood or feeling out of sorts

'I'm feeling a bit **scrungle**.'

Julie Shannon thinks this seems to sum up quite nicely the facial expressions of her kids when they are feeling unwell or out of sorts.

....

Scrunkled *adjective* a state that is between crumpled and crinkled

'I am afraid this library book has got a bit **scrunkled**.'

Gillian Bond: 'It just seemed to fill the gap between crumpled (soft) and crinkled (hard).'

....

Scuffer *noun* old man who spends most of his day in the pub drinking the cheapest bitter available. Usually wears the same clothes all week and generally smells badly. Scruffy old duffer = Scuffer

'Pub's full of **scuffers**; let's go elsewhere.'

Chris Woods says that this is widely used by anyone who has worked in a Wetherspoons pub in East London.

Scutter *noun* unpleasant person or yob. Typically someone who has no respect for others or their environment

'What a bunch of **scutters**.'

David Lynn, derived maybe from 'scum' (and 'nutter'?).

....

Shalibah *greeting* used as both hello and goodbye. Also used as a toast as in 'cheers'

'**Shalibah**, Melvyn!'

Andrew Dale and his friends think it is an old Cumbrian word meaning a sandbank but cannot be certain. They decided to use it as a greeting/toast!

....

Sharth *noun* a shower with the plug in so you can go on to wallow in the bath (or should that be shath?)

'Leave the water in the **sharth**.'

Carolyn Ovenden.

....

Shatnered *adjective* describing the mentally blank condition experienced by one person when unable to answer a simple question to which everyone else present knows the answer.

'What was the name of the actor who played 007 in the first James Bond films? I'm **shatnered**.'

Terry McArthur: 'About three years ago, playing Trivial Pursuit with friends at a dinner party I blanked when asked the name of the actor who played Captain Kirk in Star Trek. Those friends and now more, use the word "shatnered" when similarly afflicted.'

PHILIP PULLMAN
Author

The colour of scunge

All of us in the family use the word **scunge**. I first heard it on the BBC TV programme with Rod Hull and Emu when my children were young. It was on something called *EBC1: Emu's Broadcasting Company*. They talked about something being the colour of scunge. In other words it was dirty. Since then we've always used it in the family to describe something like the dirt in the bottom of a teacup or mug – something like that.

In fact, I looked up this word and it is Australian slang for 'to borrow'. Also the word 'scungy' is Australian slang for 'dirty'. Rod Hull was born in Britain, but lived for a few years in Australia. He probably brought the word over here and 'gave' it to Emu.

Another word we use is **boggits**. It was originally the mould or moss underneath the plastic roof in our lean-to beside the garage. It's used still for dirty things.

What I like about these words is that they evolve from who knows where. This is what our language is about. Most comes from the spoken language. It's interesting, though, that text language is the other way around – bottom-up as it were. It's a language which comes from being written and that basically is how it stays.

Shawl *noun* a fried egg with a broken yolk

> 'Sorry it's a **shawl** on toast today'

Anthea Hall and all of her family since the 1950s.

Sheepbutts *adjective* unfair

> 'Life's **sheepbutts**'

The Chaplins: 'Getting fed up with children always saying "It's not fair", during a car journey we compared this phrase with the rather unpleasant view of sheep's bottoms facing us as we passed, so now instead of whining we say "sheepbutts". You can't whine when you say it!'

Shillering *noun* sparkling sunlight reflected from the gently breeze-ruffled surface of a summer sea

> 'Look at that beautiful **shillering** – I could stay here for ever!'

Georgina Blake and her family use this compound of shimmer and glitter formulated by Georgina when aged five during a seaside holiday.

Shistlepot *noun* thingummyjig

> 'Where's the **shistlepot**?'

Susie Hanna: 'Freddy Whitehead was reputed to have said this word instead of "pistol shot" when performing in a Shakespeare play. It entered the family vocabulary as a replacement for forgotten words in the 1950s.'

Shizzle *exclamation* a sort of swear word meaning crap. An alternative to swearing

> '**Shizzle**! I've forgotten to do my homework again.'

Nazreen Akhter and his mates at school. 'We were in a textiles lesson and I dropped something and just happened to say shizzle, and from then on it stuck.'

Shmutz *noun* the detritus found on the chin of an animal after it has eaten.

> 'For goodness sake someone wipe the **shmutz** from her chin.'

Harry Buisseret.

Shnert *noun and verb* the noise a contented dog makes when expelling air through its nostrils to express its happiness after being given a treat.

> 'I do like to hear her **shnert** at the vicar.'

Julia Ellis and family from Warrington.

Shonk *verb* for a bus to follow closely behind the (late) bus in front, without helping pick up passengers, letting the bus in front do all the work.

> 'I've a good mind to **shonk** her all the way to Derby.'

Guy Gibson explains that bus drivers in Derbyshire and Nottinghamshire use this word. 'It, along with the term for the doer (shonker) is a derogatory term. A "shonker", who is "shonking" is seen to be avoiding work.'

Sin-in-law *noun* Live-in male partner of an unmarried daughter

> 'Jane's bringing the **sin-in-law** for Sunday lunch.'

David Tweedale.

Skadunk *noun* dog poo on pavement

> 'Watch out for the **skadunk**.'

Mandy Dewison: 'It is the sound made by a foot treading on an unwanted piece of dog waste.'

Skef *noun* an unkempt person

> 'You like look a real **skef**.'

Julia Hope.

Skiff *noun* a plastic pint glass as provided by pubs for drinking outside

> 'Anyone got a tray for me to carry these **skiffs** on?'

Caroline Luker: 'At my college (Imperial) in the late 1990s, if you took a drink outside you were asked to put it in a skiff (plastic cup). I don't know the derivation, but I have never heard the word used elsewhere.'

Slabby-gangaroot *noun* the sort of messy swarf you get around the top of an opened red-sauce bottle; general gunk

> 'Can you pass me a cloth to get rid of that **slabby-gangaroot**?'

Simon Fletcher and his colleagues at Dog House Antiques, who worry that they will find slabby-gangaroot lurking in a crevice of an old piece of furniture. Very Douglas Adams!

Slingers *noun* a meal served to visitors where there has been no shopping between the visitor's invitation and their arrival

> 'Just give them a **slingers**.'

Charles Rodney Sabine, invented by Granny Sabine (presumably to show her displeasure for the lack of preparation by other cooks in the Sabine family?).

Slobstopper *noun* a baby's bib

> 'Time to put your **slobstopper** on, Grandad!'

David Nutt, because it sounds so much more expressive than 'bib'.

Sloindez *noun* a break from university studying, spent indulging in football on the Playstation, usually coinciding with lunchtime or when *Neighbours* is on, whichever is sooner.

'Time for a **sloindez**.'

Chris Awcock and his fellow students: 'Whilst studying at Southampton University my friends and I would use football on the Playstation for breaks in revision and essay-writing. The word sloindez comes from a Japanese version of Pro Evo Football we found. Every time the ball went out of play the commentator shouted out SLOINDEZ!

....

Slonk *verb* to stay in bed long after you have actually woken up from the night's sleep. Generally characterised by intermittent dozing and refusing instructions to get out of bed. The short definition would be an overly indulgent and unjustifiable lie-in. Also referred to as **slooming**

'I see John's **slonking** again.'

Simon Ward: 'In permanent use in my childhood as successive siblings went through adolescence. Particularly well used when there are teenagers around.' Also used by Gillian Gabbatt in the more general sense of lying around idly watching TV.

....

Slosher *noun* an individual who does not socialise or go partying

'She's not really a **slosher**.'

Kieran Quince and a growing number of friends in the Luton-Dunstable area. 'It was first used when a friend was asleep, a funny word that popped out and grew from there, and is becoming wildly more popular.'

Kitchen Table Lingo across the UK – where some of the words come from

Ladgin – Yorkshire

Lah-loo – Ireland

Leuchars Junction Question – Fife, Scotland

Liverpolitan – Liverpool

Loishing – Devon

Lun – Salisbury

Melly – Ireland

Mim – Stratford and London

Nesh – Stoke-on-Trent

Nibbygorger – Kent

Noffage – Hertfordshire

Nonge – Cambridge

Noofle – Gloucestershire

Northsouthers – London

Oggsnitch – Hertfordshire

Schneb – Wales

Slosher – Luton/Dunstable

Snudge – South Wales

Splig – North Wales

Spraff – Edinburgh/Lothian

Tudorbungacot – Chislehurst

Umfti – Isle of Wight

Wafty – Suffolk

Weakers – North Wales

Wesleybob – Bradford

Willakey – Kent

Slother *verb* to drag one's feet across the ground instead of walking properly

'Stop **slothering**!'

Gren Gaskell and the good people of Bulwell.

....

Slub *noun* a casserole-type meal made up without a recipe, often using leftovers

'This **slub** is delicious.'

Jeremy Iles.

....

Slutchy *adjective* feeling off-colour and generally unwell without a specific cause

'I just feel a bit **slutchy**.'

David Brown and the GOSW IT team (whose systems are never **slutchy** but always **avlexly**!).

....

Smeesh *verb* describes the action of gently squeezing the soft area of the tummy in a gesture of affection (particularly for young children and babies)

'Just **smeesh** Alice, that normally settles her down.'

The Moran family.

Smockraffle *verb* to consume food greedily and speedily, usually without consideration for others

'He certainly **smockraffled** that meal down.'

Susan Le Gras and people in Lincolnshire or Yorkshire, possibly merchant navy slang.

....

Snart *noun* a tough bit of food that you can't chew or eat and put on the side of the plate.

'Just leave the **snart** on the side of your plate.'

Chris Harris.

....

Snerfy *adjective* itchy or irritating, causing discomfort

'This shirt's so **snerfy**.'

Edward Ashworth: 'As a small child when my mother dressed me in something like lambswool and it was itchy, it was my word to tell her it was uncomfortable. It is still used by our family and extended family (I am now twenty-eight).'

....

Snergle *verb* the action of a cat pushing its head against you

'I love it when Tiddles **snergles** me like that.'

Sally French, her immediate family, and various cat-lovers.

Snickersnack *noun and adjective* mischievous or naughty, applied to an action or person

> 'That was a **snickersnack** thing to do.'

Mark Guest coined this as a young child twenty years ago and it is currently used by members of his extended family (who presumably also enjoyed galumphing through Lewis Carroll's 'Jabberwocky' when young).

Snoozy-watch *noun and verb* (to have) a nap in front of the TV

> 'Ah good. *Neighbours*. I'll just have a little **snoozy-watch**!'

Harriet Hopkinson.

Snotfair *noun* an interview with a university student who is unhappy with a grade or mark given for an assignment, believing it to be an unfair assessment in relation to the amount of effort expended.

> 'Got to go and have my weekly **snotfair** with my class.'

Gill Christy and her academic colleagues. 'Possibly originates from Sue Limb's "Dulcie Domum" column in the *Guardian* some years back, but also reflects the common expression of the complaint, viz. "It's not fair, I worked really hard and only got 52 per cent."'

Snudge *verb* prodding, nudging movement made by a dog with its nose when it wants your attention

> 'Tehya's **snudging** me again, it must be time for a walk.'

Kim Dowdell, Steve (and their dogs Tehya and Takoda) in South Wales. Also Rachel Offley, whose dog prefers the more refined **snurge** when it rubs its nose on the carpet!

....

Sopholargic *adjective* pleasantly tired and relaxed

> 'I feel nicely **sopholargic**.'

BJ Meridew, to describe the 'combination of soporific and lethargic, neither of which fully describes the feelings of this now quite frequently used word'.

....

Soupdragon *noun* liquidiser

> 'I'll just mix them up in the **soupdragon**.'

Chris Hazlegrove, who purchased one at the time *The Clangers* first appeared on TV.

....

Spiggy *noun* fool, idiot

> 'He's such a **spiggy**.'

Hilary Derby and family in a kind/unkind sort of a way . . .

Splig *noun and adjective* the pointed shapes made when, for example, the two slices of a sandwich of thickly buttered bread are pulled apart. Leads to: **splig-like** or **spliggy**, which can be applied to any irregularly pointed object

'The Matterhorn looks distinctly **spliggy**.'

Danny Grimwood, trying to find a word to describe the shape of Cnicht, a mountain in Snowdonia.

Splonker *noun* TV remote control

'Let someone else use the **splonker**.'

Kate Shorts and friends in North-West London

Splosh *noun* tea

'I'm dying for a cup of **splosh**.'

Katina, from the sound tea makes when you pour it.

Spoffle *verb* to gobble

'Who **spoffled** all the biscuits?'

Morey family.

KATHY LETTE

Australian-born novelist and wit

Sex, private lingo and the president of Liechtenstein!

I left school at sixteen – the only examination I passed is my cervical smear test. I'm also an autodidact, which is itself a word I taught myself. So it means I can break the rules, mainly because I don't know there are any.

Most of my private lingo was invented during girl talk with gal pals. As sexism is innate in the language, women have always invented codewords to describe our wild and wicked ways without alerting prudes to our promiscuity. Among my girlfriends we all know and use these words:

Stick-sisters: two women who have slept with the same man. However there is a connotation here of cama-raderie than rivalry.

Wide-on: this is our female version of a 'hard-on'. In other words, it is used to describe a woman getting excited and drooling over some man, which would give her a 'wide-on'. I'm sure you can work out why.

Liechtenstein: this is our coded reference to cunnilingus. I'm sure you can work out the 'lick' bit. Like 'Did he do Liechtenstein?' To which the reply might be: 'He's the president of Liechtenstein.'

I'm told too that the *OED* has only excised one phrase – 'new man'. The people at the *OED* realised that it is a male myth. It is only men who called themselves 'new men', and that was in the hope of getting a bonk!'

Spraff *verb and noun* to spraff (also **spraff on**) to talk nonsense. Someone can also be described as a **spraff** if they are known to talk rubbish a lot

> 'Turn the radio off, Tam, I can't bear to hear him **spraffing** so much.'

Samantha Clair: 'I heard it first at secondary school, thinking it was a word coined there, but when I moved to Glasgow I found that other people from Edinburgh/Lothian and the surrounding areas used it as well. It has since been spread (at the very least) among those people from outside of Edinburgh that I went to university with!' Just the kind of word for politicians to use about the West Lothian question?

....

Spreethy *adjective* refers to a mild form of chapped skin, mainly on the legs, caused by exposure to cold weather

> 'Have you got some cream? My hands are all **spreethy**.'

Eileen Avis and family in Walthamstow, since the 1950s.

....

Spurgler *noun* remote control

> 'Chuck me the **spurgler**, please'

Earl O'Keefe, somewhere between a switch, a purge and a burglar!

....

Squimp *verb* to slop a liquid over the edge of something, such as tea out of a teacup into the saucer

> 'Björn, you've **squimped** your beer all over the record sleeve.'

Ingemar Hunnings: 'Possibly from a Swedish word of similar meaning as my mother is Swedish and the word came from her.'

Squirmish *adjective* how you feel when you have the unpleasant but not quite nauseous feeling you get in your stomach when you see or think of things that make you feel uncomfortable, such as eye operations or having stitches in very sensitive parts of the body

'Look away if you are feeling **squirmish**.'

Ashworth family, in a nice mixture of squeamish and squirm.

Squirter *noun* remote control

'Who's got the **squirter**?'

Nick Fisher.

Suggston *noun* a suggestion that is actually a command

'My **suggston** is that we all stop what we are doing and go for a walk.'

Simon Greenly and his extended family 'from the concept of the iron fist in the velvet glove – a polite way of saying "do this"'.

Swamble *noun and verb* the act of being engulfed by a large group of people walking together and towards you, often tourists in a tour group. Slow speed and high density are necessary for the people to count as **swamblers**, the name for a person who swambles

'Look out, **swamble** alert!'

Thomas George.

The story behind **squinker**

Squinker *noun* a baby

As a well-known writer Anne Atkins feeds off words. 'We're a verbose family,' she says. So experimenting with words is a staple of family life with her five children. 'We play word games all the time as a family, such as Reverse Tennis Elbow, Just a Minute and Pass the Poem,' she explains. (Pass the Poem is when you have to create the next few lines of a continuous poem, while making it as difficult as possible for the person after you to complete the rhyme.) 'It's usually around the kitchen table. I think that's important, because it's mostly while eating together – and drinking, actually – that these things happen.' The melding together of a close family life, having meals and being creative with language, is all part of a continuum.

Noun, verb, adjective

The Atkins family has contributed two words to this book of Kitchen Table Lingo. **Horserubbish** (for horse-radish) came from outside the family but has lodged itself into regular usage in the Atkins household. It is the kind of anarchic, irreverent word which forms part of the core of family humour and which helps to bind people together. But **squinker** is home-grown by Bink, one of Anne's daughters.

'We've got zillions of our own family words,' says Bink. 'For example, there's **bishbosh** meaning toothpaste, and **squonk** meaning hello – although it's much better than hello. **Squonk** in effect says, "We need a pointless greeting here, so here we go: **Squonk**."

'I came up with **squinker**, meaning baby, for my little sister when she was born. At first it was a verb: to **squink**, meaning the way tiny babies squirm, squint up their eyes, and do that thing with their fingers when they stretch them out and wiggle them. Then it became an adjective because she was such a **squinkety** little thing. From there it was soon a common noun, **squinker**, meaning baby (or small child); while Rosie herself is now **Squinker** or **The Squinker**, a proper noun. So we might say, "How many **squinkers** will be at **The Squinker's** birthday party?" or even, "You're being very **squinkety**, **Squinker**; stop **squinking** if you want this necklace on." Though, obviously, we wouldn't really use the same word so often in one sentence.'

'It's when people have a framework of grammar that they can extend the meaning of a word into other uses,' says Anne. 'To be creative you need to know the rules – and then feel free to break them.'

Swoop *noun* a cross between stew and soup

> 'I see they're setting up a **swoop** kitchen in Mayfair for the hedge-funders.'

Alexandra Curling and family.

....

Swuggle *verb* to swish around in water, e.g. hand-washing, adding bath lotion

> 'I'll just **swuggle** my hands.'

Carol Watson: 'Passed down from my mother and used when doing washing by hand, etc.'

....

Add your own KTL word here

word   _____

definition   _____

sample   _____

             _____

T

Taffle *noun* a tangle or knot in the hair

'It's time to take the **taffles** out of my dreads.'

Rosie Webb and her family.

Taited *verb* the action of a rugby player being picked up and carried by a tackler

'I was **taited** and touched down.'

Gareth Parsons and Welsh rugby supporters who recall that this was coined after the 2005 Wales v England rugby international.

Tanatanatat *noun* a cash register or till

'Does your **tanatanatat** accept plastic?'

Laura Barber and family members, who point out it was invented in a moment of onomatopoeic ingenuity in the late 1970s by a three-year-old sister 'who was trying to describe what she wanted for Christmas by making the noise made by the shop-keeper tapping in the price and the till roll printing out'. We hope to keep plenty of tanatanatats busy ourselves this year.

Tangersuma *noun* an all-purpose word for small, round orange fruit of unspecified type – tangerine, satsuma, clementine, etc

> 'I see we've got **tangersuma** peel all over the kitchen table as usual!'

Dr Paul Jonathan Fray and family, who admit that the word was necessitated as a result of a congenital inability to distinguish these fruits one from the other. Hence the hybrid word.

Tansad *noun* pushchair, baby buggy

> 'Your turn to take the **tansad**.'

Tim O'Brien and family, who say it is current in Lancashire and the north of England.

Tapoes *noun* potatoes

> 'A kilo o' **tapoes**, please.'

Jonathan Ferris, together with parents, grandparents and brother. 'I couldn't say the word potatoes and was convinced that a potato was a tapoe for many years.' It took root.

Tappitt *noun* a young person who has their music booming and car windows all open

> 'Alert! **Tappitts** sighted at twelve o'clock.'

Su Edwards and her fellow sufferers.

Tardpack *noun* a person who does something astoundingly stupid, despite being told not to.

> 'Paris is such a **tardpack**!'

Jason Stone of the USA and a small number of internet users who devised it from the nickname for the Microsoft Xbox 360 console that was sold cheap and missing critical features.

Telly box *noun* remote control

> 'The superglue has squirted all over the **telly box**.'

Ed Tunnacliffe and Paul Beard.

Terrid *adjective* cross between terrible and horrid

> 'Was it **terrid** or just plain awful?'

Andree Bramley-Little, who uses it with her husband and daughter but says it is extending to the wider family.

Testiculate *verb* to wave one's arms about while talking bollocks

> 'The ability to **testiculate** has now become mandatory – rather than merely desirable – for the job of Chancellor.'

Pete Davison, who says it was created by Cedric Shute, retired curator of palaeobotany at the Natural History Museum, to describe the wafflings of certain colleagues and the palaeobotanists. Now apparently popular with drinkers in pubs around South Kensington. Also submitted by Tony Green and regular pub-goers.

Thangy *adjective* applied to underpants past their wear-by date.

> 'How long before Victoria's thong goes **thangy**?'

David Wakeford and his family, who invented a version of Scrabble in which the words must not be in the *Oxford English Dictionary* but must be plausible entries. The player placing the word had to give its meaning. Thangy was coined in this context. 'We use thangy underwear for cleaning and dusting,' adds David. An important lesson in economy for all of us, times being what they are.

Threewards *adverb* backwards (as in direction of DVD, videos, etc)

> 'I always watch my football DVDs **threewards**.'

Jo Stonehouse and family, inspired by son who used the word aged two. 'I need to make it go threewards.'

Tinkle tonkles *noun* Christmas tree decorations

> 'Let's put the Kitchen Table Lingo book under the **tinkle tonkles**.'

Susan Hornby and family, who say the word is derived from 'the noise made when hanging them'.

Tinky-toot *noun* remote control

> 'The **tinky-toot** has tanked.'

Jessica RW Johnson.

Tinsellitis *noun* the rage you feel at Christmas due to inflated shop prices and extra long shop queues.

> 'Doctor, doctor, I keep wanting to smash Father Christmas over the head with a plastic reindeer; do I have **tinsellitis**?'

Rachel Wallace: 'I coined it as we seemed to have all sorts of other rage covered except Christmas!'

Tisty-tosty *noun* fir cone

> 'We need some **tisty-tosty** and glitter under the tree.'

Craig Murray, his sister and parents: 'It was a word used to describe a fir cone to me as a child – we still use it!'

Trancliments *noun* tools or accessories required for professional use

> 'She had left her **trancliments** all over the place.'

Allan Emmott, who says it is used by tradesmen and professionals. 'A friend of mine, John Hasch, has used the word for the last twenty years in relation to our police equipment, such as handcuffs, truncheon, pocket book, etc, and now in civilian life we use it when we go out, relating to a mobile phone, wallet, comb, etc.' Also contributed by Len Breeze, **trankliments** –useful bits and pieces of equipment; and as **tranklements** by Cresby Brown on behalf of the Ingram family, who say it means frippery, encumbrance, paraphernalia; and John Etheridge, who says it means bits and pieces, odds and ends. John Etheridge adds that he thinks 'the word derives from the glove-making industry in Walsall, where the trank was the bits of leather left over after the glove was cut from the sheet'.

Trebus *noun* unnecessary possessions, clutter, junk, bric-a-brac taking up valuable space. Recent impulse purchases that have no use

> 'Right, Francesca, your room is full of **trebus**. It's got to go.'

Julian Harrison and family and friends inspired by a Mr Trebus, an eccentric Pole, who never threw anything away.

....

Tudge *verb* to push in a helpful manner

> 'If I **tudge** him he'll resign.'

Pete Laity and his close family.

....

Tudorbungacot *noun* a horrible new-build house that subscribes to no single genre of architecture but many

> 'At least the credit crunch means fewer **tudorbunga-cots**.'

Sue Turner and graphics students. 'My first degree was at Ravensbourne College of Art, Chislehurst,' says Sue. 'The place was littered with them. A place of bad taste for people with more money than taste. But then the two generally go together.' Please note that, to avoid offence, residents of Chislehurst should have looked away by now.

ROSIE MILLARD
Newspaper columnist and broadcaster

Millard family lingo

Having your own 'lingo' at home is part of being in a big family. If you are an only child, there is no hope of special 'in' words ricocheting around via other siblings, and any such language would in any case fall prey to parent filter, which would kill it stone dead. As one of four, special words could be wholly incubated between us children before they emerged, fully formed, at the dining table. Soon our parents would start using them. And indeed, thirty years on, we all still do.

Soup 'n' bones: what we would always eat on Sunday nights. Usually consisted of a boiled egg and nothing else. Context: 'What's for supper?' '**Soup 'n' bones**.' 'Oh!'

Extraction time: moment when my father would drag us all out of bed; we would usually be shouting curses at him. Preluded by fierce clapping up the stairs and singing of phrase '**Extraction time**' quite loudly.

Last bark: derived from family dog who would always respond to orders to shut up by barking a low-level woofing noise. Since then used to define person who always has to have last say in an argument (usually Mr Millard). Context: 'Whoa! Don't give me the last bark!'

The BBC is of course like a rather maladjusted family and has developed its own lingua franca. With both my husband and me working there, we could have a totally comprehensible conversation wholly in White City lingo, for example, **disco**, a discussion, usually around a table in a studio. 'We're having a **disco** tonight with Jeremy Paxman and Arthur Scargill,' was the phrase which greeted my husband on Day One at *Newsnight*. Sadly it wasn't the funky *Saturday Night Fever* experience he was expecting.

Goldfishing: when the sound is cut from a talking head so they are allowed to open and shut their mouth mindlessly.

And **Lord Privy Seal**: criticism of literal writing, or when a (badly written) script exactly echoes the pictures on screen, as in phrase 'lord privy seal' to run along pictures of a lord, a loo, and a performing seal. To be avoided at all costs.

Clawth-ez: Ukrainian pronunciation of 'clothes', meaning overcoat. Picked up by Mr Millard when he was filming in the Ukraine and now used between us for any item of clothing. Context: 'Can you put your Clawth-ez in the cupboard?'

Twirly or **twerly** *noun* a senior citizen who wants to take advantage of off-peak travel and travel as early as possible

> 'I had six **twerlys** in the back of my bus this morning.'

Steve Bannister, David Peck and bus drivers. 'It comes from them asking the drivers "Am I too early?" Also from Denise Hollands.

Twinquisition *noun* the experience of being questioned in the street and elsewhere by random strangers about newborn twins

> 'I had a full **twinquisition** this morning – and no time off for their good behaviour.'

Claire Summerfield and other parents of twins who have become inured to being bombarded by questions related to their twins.

Add your own KTL word here

word _____

definition _____

sample _____

_____

Remote control

There was no doubt about it. Liz was **frangled**. She **frabbed** with her mobile, checking she was getting reception. Suddenly a voice spoke in her *earslug*. 'Let's go. Meet you in five minutes as agreed.'

Liz walked briskly down the road, avoiding a **gheeney** sitting on the pavement but pausing momentarily to admire a **hench** workman setting up scaffolding. Then she stopped to let a couple of early morning **gidders** amble past, arm in arm.

She could feel her heart beating just like it did on a gleehueham day. For a moment she felt quite **gwaggly**.

'What the **hammershaft**! You gave me a fright, Polly.'

'Sorry. I just don't want to be late.'

The two women walked on briskly, each privately excited by the naughtiness of their *hokum*.

Later that evening, feeling pleasantly **sopholargic**, Liz poured them both large gin and tonics. There on the carpet were the fruits of their highly successful mission. Ishes. A lovely *cosy coat*. So much wonderful trebus. Always good to be early for the January sales.

'Look at the time. Guy will be home soon. Better remove the evidence!'

'Why, will he ask?'

'I doubt it. It's a kind of **Leuchars Junction Question**.'

At which point the umfti rang. It was Guy. 'Darling. Terribly sorry. Something's come up. I won't be back until late. Don't wait up.'

Liz turned to Polly. 'Looks like we have a night on our own. Let's see if there's a good film on. Pass me the . . .'

U

Uckers *noun* sausages

'If you're down on your luck there's nothing like a plate of **uckers** and chips to cheer you up.'

Leslie Nurden: 'My grandfather was frying some sausages when asked by someone what he was frying. He replied, "**Uckers** because you uck them in uck them over and uck them out".'

Umbumbatious *adjective* stroppy, bad-tempered

'Now she's a teenager she's so **umbumbatious**.'

Christine Adams, invented by her husband.

Umfti *noun* telephone

'Les, someone on the **umfti** for you.'

Les Cooper, his family and 'stupid friends'. Les is from the Isle of Wight which, he says, explains everything. Curious!

V

Vibble *noun* small rodent or nose of a small rodent

'See the **vibble** wriggle.'

Richard, Helen and Lucie Taylor, who explain it is derived from the Saarland German dialectal verb *wibbeln*, which means to twitch.

Visipants *noun* underwear deliberately on display due to low-cut trousers (especially teenagers')

'I see **visipants** are big in Milan again this year.'

Liz Cantle and family (who do not reveal whether or not they wear them).

Vom-vod *noun* the towel used to catch vomit when burping babies over your shoulder

'Quick, pass me the **vom-vod**.'

Sabine Tillie Davidson's UK and Belgium family. 'It originated with my Belgian family,' says Sabine. 'There is a real need for such a word.' So another useful Belgian import, like chocolate and beer then.

Votergenic *adjective* possessing the characteristics that will appeal to voters

> 'Mirror, mirror on the wall, who's the most **votergenic** of all?'

Martyn Park and close family and friends when discussing political candidates. 'I was looking for a word to describe why I thought Tony Blair should be chosen as the Labour leader,' recalls Martyn. 'I came up with votergenic – after photogenic – in that he had characteristics that would make him appealing to voters.'

Add your own KTL word here

word _____

definition _____

sample _____

_____

W

Wafty *noun* something that is old, too large, inefficient, broken or not being used for its intended purpose

'That car is pretty **wafty**!'

William Hatch, and used by James Diaper, Tobias Phillips, Giles Orford, Rowan Orford, Ollie Diaper, Rob Fellowes, Steph Smith, Helen Rowley and more . . . 'This word was coined by a late Will Hatch. It was used in conversation to describe an old, decrepit van that we were driving as part of a delivery. The van would continually break down and was too large for what we needed it for. The word quickly spread amongst our group of friends and further afield, as a word to describe old, fragile vehicles/machinery.'

Wallock *noun* a mallet for hammering in tent pegs

'Pass me the **wallock**, please.'

Lisle Rider: 'Nearly twenty years ago my son, when aged about seven, invented this name for the instrument he was using for banging in tent pegs, and we have adopted its use ever since.'

Wanger *noun* remote control

'Wang me the **wanger**, please.'

Victoria Wood.

Wayo *noun* fire engine

> 'Watch out for the **wayo**.'

Christina Corr.

Wazziebazine *noun* washing machine

> 'Oh no! The cat's going round and round in the **wazziebazine** again.'

Patricia Riley.

Weakers *noun* ears

> 'Keep your **weakers** open for any useful information.'

Liz Thompson: 'We think that this word originated from my grandmother, Madelaine Jude.'

Wesleybob *noun* a Christmas tree bauble

> 'Aren't those **wesleybobs** pretty?'

Andrea Crabtree.

Whimpet *noun* a moany, clingy child

> 'For goodness' sake leave that **whimpet** and come and join us for lunch!'

'Mark', combining whimper plus limpet.

Whizzywash *noun* launderette

> 'Anyone got a pound coin for the **whizzywash**?'

Andrew McClellan and friends in Liverpool. 'Assume it's because it was faster than doing it by hand.'

See also **wazziebazine**

Wicky *noun* a sudden pain in a hip joint so that your leg gives way

> 'Ouch. Just felt a **wicky**.'

Katherine Sharples and her family. She explains: 'I get words muddled and this one has stuck for about twenty years. I have hip pains and now the other members of my family use it.'

Widger *noun* remote control

> 'This **widger**'s wafty. I'll just have to get up and turn the TV off myself!'

Mike Willans.

Wigglepush *noun* wire tie used to fasten plastic food bags

> 'Where are all the **wigglepushes**?'

Carolyn Kennian, whose great-aunt made it up thirty-five years ago.

Wilbergraph *noun* a photograph where the subject is so far away it is almost impossible to make out what it is

> 'Typical **wilbergraph**: can't see what the hell I'm meant to be looking at.'

Jim Elliott 'from an old family friend of my father-in-law, Colonel Hugh Wilberforce, who used to take many such photos'.

Willakey *noun* a weak person who gives in to pressure – as in the US word flaky

> 'He's just too **willakey** to rely on.'

Eve Olley in Kent.

Wimble *verb* to procrastinate over something, to defer or put something off. Also used to indicate lazing or idling around or mumbling incoherently

> 'Stop **wimbling** and get on with it!'

Craig Lovelace: 'Generally used during childhood. The actual word is a device used in drilling so taken totally out of context by my family.'

Winky *adjective* bitter or sour, so much so that it makes you blink, especially an apple

'Yuk. This apple's so **winky**.'

Avril Nash and Valerie Moore.

Wirrel *noun* the upper part of the hindquarters of a cat that forms an arch when it is sitting with all its legs tucked underneath it

'I think that's what you call a **wirrel**.'

Hilary Brown.

Wishya *noun* a word describing something you wished you had not done or said

'How embarrassing. That was a real **wishya**.'

Andrew Bywater.

Wiz-wiz *noun* TV remote control

'Where's the **wiz-wiz**? It's time for *Newsnight*.'

Brod Mason.

Wizgigging *verb* to laugh uncontrollably, particularly used in relation to children

'If they don't stop **wizgigging** they'll never go to bed!'

Hazel Derham: 'My father used it when we were children at the meal table when something would make us laugh and nothing could stop us, since using the word would make us laugh even more.' That's Kitchen Table Lingo for you.

....

Wizzle *verb* to whine or moan

'For heaven's sake, stop **wizzling** and face the facts!'

JES Bradshaw says that this onomatopoeic word came 'from the noise made by a particularly vocal British Toggenburg goat we owned at the time'.

....

Wollocks *adjective* describes when things have gone awry

'The Labour party's **wollocks**!'

Sandra Ayres.

....

Womsie *adjective* childishly amusing or fascinating

'Aren't they just **womsie**?'

John Nicholson.

....

Wrobble *adjective* something that is all crinkled, scrunched up

'Have you got an iron? My clothes are **wrobble**.'

Adam Roberts in Worcestershire.

JEREMY VINE

Broadcaster and presenter of his own Radio 2 show

Watch out for wombles, squiffles, grollies and, of course, Humptydumpty!

I've got various words:

Squiffle: this is a verb meaning 'to hide, to sneak or to squash' something, usually into a small space. I've used it for years in the context of, say, 'I squiffled the tennis balls into the little bag.' I think I have used it because it simply sounds just right.

Grollies: these are testicles. I might say it like 'the boxer Ricky Hatton went down after the other guy hit him in the grollies.' I heard it used at Hull when I was there more than twenty years ago at university. I've simply kept it but have no idea how widespread it is.

Wombled: I use it to mean 'drunk'. It just sounds good. I guess it is because drunk people maybe wobbling or maybe it came from *The Wombles*. I've also heard teenagers use it.

Humptydumpty: it means something 'gone wrong or broken'. You can see that it comes from the nursery rhyme as 'Humpty Dumpty had a great fall'. I heard it used years ago by the football manager and commentator Ron Atkinson who said of a team that it had 'gone all Humpty Dumpty'. I liked it and have since used it myself and within the family.

Y

....

Yampy *adjective* a bit crazy or mad

'You cannot be serious! In fact, you must be **yampy**!'

Richard Morris and friends in Worcester.

....

Yumpty *noun* a small, special treat or gift

'Darling. Here's a little **yumpty** from me, with my love.'

Sarah Milne.

....

Yupes *noun* male underpants

'Bradshaw. Take those **yupes** off your head now and put your cap on.'

JES Bradshaw and officer cadets at Sandhurst. 'I understand this originated at Welbeck College and derives from the letters UPS, standing for underpants!' Cripes!

Z

....

Zabazar *noun* pushchair

   'Can we put the zebra in the **zabazar**?'

Venetia Horton, who, having coined the word as a child, now
uses it with the Harrison and Horton families.

....

Add your own KTL word here

word _____

definition _____

sample _____

_____

The story behind **zanden**

Zanden *adjective* anything triangular in shape

Mo Farrell contributed a number of words to the Kitchen Table Lingo collection but the one that stood out for us was **zanden**, meaning triangle. It is a powerful, forceful word in its own right, but its added interest is that it was invented by Tom, her son, when aged not much more than an infant.

'Word-making and wordplay is in the blood,' says Mo, a journalist while Nigel Farrell, Tom's dad, is a well-known broadcaster. 'My father was a genius when it came to making up new words, and there are lots of family words which have been handed on down the generations. Another family favourite is **dod**, which means cute. When my second husband heard it first he was quite bemused by it, but now he has taken it up and uses it as a normal part of his vocabulary.'

Whereas many Kitchen Table Lingo words have an onomatopoeic inspiration, **zanden** is very unusual because it stems from the visual correlation between the capital letters N and Z and the shape of the object it represents. We'll have to find out whether there is a word for that.

Afterword

DAVID CRYSTAL

Author, broadcaster and expert on English language

The words in this book are the tip of an unexplored linguistic iceberg. Who knows how many private and personal word creations there are in a language? But one thing is certain: they are there, in every household and in every social group, and everyone has been a word-coiner at some time or other, if not around the kitchen table, then in the garden, bedroom, office or pub.

Linguists have long studied these neologisms as part of research into children's acquisition of language. Anyone with young kids knows how fascinating their playful word coinages can be. The rest of the family then pick up these cute forms, and they become part of a domestic tradition. As you'd expect, linguists have devised a technical term for these dialects of the home: they call them *familects*.

But it isn't just children who invent such words.

As this book shows, coinages can come from anyone, of any age and background. Indeed, no species is exempt, as Tigger (of *Winnie the Pooh* fame) illustrates with his penchant for such blends as *prezactly* (precisely + exactly). Lewis Carroll was a great inventor of neologisms, especially in 'Jabberwocky'. It is even possible to make a showbiz living out of them, as Stanley Unwin did: remember his 'Goldiloppers and the Three Bearloders'?

Some newspapers and radio programmes have competitions for invented words. The *Washington Post* has a famous one, and I remember one on the Terry Wogan show years ago. When I was presenting *English Now* for Radio 4 in the 1980s, I held a competition in which listeners sent in their favourite examples of home-grown words. The producer and I expected the usual postbag of a couple of hundred cards. That week we got over a thousand. It confirmed my belief that everyone has a linguistic story to tell.

The words in this book may be new, but the processes of word formation that they use are not. Forms such as **bimbensioner** illustrate a standard way of making new words – by blending existing words. Some (such as **bingle**) tap into the ancient phonetic properties of the language. Most inventions will stay private, personal and unknown. Very occasionally, one or two will prove popular and end up as a permanent addition to the language – but, of course, only if people hear about them. That could be one of the surprising consequences of reading this book.

Why not become a part of the Kitchen Table Lingo Community?

If you have enjoyed *Kitchen Table Lingo* then there is plenty more on offer and opportunities for you to take part.

Visit www.englishproject.org/ktl where you will find exciting developments including:

✓ word leagues
✓ competitions
✓ trivia
✓ facts and figures

We very much welcome your views on any of the words in this book. Do tell us if you have come across them before, especially if you use them with different meanings.

And, of course, you can contribute your Kitchen Table Lingo for 2009!

We look forward to seeing you there.

Kitchen Table Lingo is a signature event for The English Project, bringing out the fun and the richness of the English language.